DISCIPLINES
of the
H · O · M · E

Anne Ortlund

WORD PUBLISHING

Dallas · London · Vancouver · Melbourne

DISCIPLINES OF THE HOME

Library of Congress Cataloging-in-Publication Data

Ortlund, Anne.
    Disciplines of the home / Anne Ortlund.
        p. cm.
    ISBN 0–8499–0678–4
            0–8499–3518–0 (tp)
        1. Family. 2. Family-Religious life. I. Title.
HQ518.O78   1990
306.85—dc20   89–70765
                                                                                      CIP

Printed in the United States of America

3 4 5 6 9   LB   9 8 7 6 5 4 3 2 1

To

My beloved Ray;

Sherry and Walt,
        Mindy,
        Beth Anne,
        Drew;
Margie and John,
        Lisa,
        Laurie,
        John IV;
Ray, Jr., and Jani,
        Eric,
        Krista,
        Dane,
        Gavin;
Nels

C O N T E N T S

PORTRAIT:
Let's begin with a model.

THE THREAT:
We've lost the world of Joe and Betty Sweet,
and we can't ever get it back.

*Today's society is an impending
avalanche sliding toward hell.
Is your family caught in the slide?
How can you gather up your
loved ones and make a drastic
leap to solid ground?*

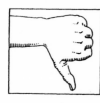

TWO DRASTIC DON'TS:

1. DON'T RETREAT. Don't try to go

2. DON'T DIVORCE from now on,
whatever your past. Let's look at

TEN DRASTIC DO'S:

1. DO SLOW DOWN. Make brave, radical
cuts in everybody's schedules. You need
less money, more time, more exposure

2. DO "BE THERE"—one parent or the
other or both, until the kids are

INTRODUCTION

We used to have Sunday dinner sometimes at Rosemary and Alfred's. The table was always beautifully set; the food was always delicious; and best of all, we were so warmly welcomed! We were always truly wanted.

And so were a ninety-five-year-old man who drooled a lot, and a blind lady, and a very fat lady, and others. People at Alfred and Rosemary's table weren't invited because they were classy but because they were genuinely loved.

God's circle is like that. It's a tender, warm, nourishing place for all kinds of people—some of us not too bright, some smart but without much courage when the chips are down, some good-looking but pretty stupid—everybody a little funny, one way or another.

But whatever, one thing is certain: the Lord really loves and wants us. He enjoys helping us improve and making us happy. He desires us around His table. We don't have to stand off in a corner, we don't have to eat in the kitchen— we belong. We have a place. We're welcome.

Is your home anything like that?

Probably you've got some kind of combination of bodies under your roof: you're a married couple with no kids, a married couple with kids, a single mom or dad with kids; maybe some parents are with you or foster kids or grandchildren—you know your own setup. Ogden Nash says a family unit is composed not only of children but of men, women, an occasional animal, and the common cold.

The big questions aren't, How sharp are all of you? and, How much money are you making?

The big questions—no matter how odd your assortment or what their histories or deformities or problems—the big questions are . . .

How do you get along?

How do you help each other and lift each other?

Is your home a place where your young ones can get prepared for tomorrow's world?

Your old ones get comforted?

Your unwise ones get tender guidance?

Your producers get recharged?

Your hurt ones healed?

Or if God has included under your roof any of His lambs who are truly inadequate for this world—is home still where they're loved, where they know they belong?

In other words, is your home a restoring, nourishing, comforting, inspiring place?

God's is, and He wants yours to be.

I'm excited, writing this book. The need is so great, and God has such powerful solutions!

Maybe you've already read *Disciplines of the Beautiful Woman,* for help in living your external life for God: using a notebook, keeping a desk, organizing your wardrobe.

Then you may have read *Disciplines of the Heart* for help with your interior—your heart life, thought life, between-the-ears life.

(Some people said to me recently, "Anne, in the first book you threw rubber-tipped darts at us. In the second one you used knives!" Oh, dear.)

But "no man or woman is an island," as they say. And when my friends at Word Publishing asked that I make the "disciplines" books a trilogy, with this third one on the home, I was glad to say yes.

This book, too, has study suggestions. Maybe you'll want to gather a group and study all three books in a series—hopefully for a triple whammy.

May God greatly lift your sights and give you new visions of what your very own home can become for Him—"a restoring, nourishing, comforting, inspiring place."

# Portrait: Joe and Betty Sweet

Joe and Betty met in 1914 under a tree. Rural, Irish Catholic Joe, strongly built but not handsome, immediately fell in love with gorgeous, dark, willowy, Presbyterian Mary Elizabeth Weible—a city girl, delicately raised. The tree was on the campus of Kansas State Agricultural College, where Joe had struggled to pay for every minute of his so far two years of studies, and Mary was a new freshman fully supported by her family.

Joe was to be my father, and Mary, my mother. But at that point they couldn't have been more different—too different to be suitable to marry each other.

Joe's birthplace had been a nice two-story family home in Denver, which his gambling father lost soon after little Joe was born. Moving to a small farm to begin again, Joe's father and mother both slowly sickened with tuberculosis and eventually left their four young sons and two tiny daughters orphans to fend for themselves.

Was Joe the "Cinderella"? The other boys had their father's dashing good looks; the little girls were beautiful; Joe was homely. In any case, it was eleven-year-old Joe, third of the four boys, who dropped out of school to farm and care for the two little sisters and help put his brothers through college.

1

Ten schoolless years later, when the boys had their diplomas and the girls were situated in homes as domestic help, Joe himself started back to school, crammed junior high and high school subjects to pass an entrance exam, and put himself through college as well.

The third fall on campus, when Joe saw incoming freshman Mary Weible under that tree—for him, everything was new. He proved to her his worth through outrageous effort: he worked both day- and night-jobs, he got straight A's, and he became colonel of the college R.O.T.C. And from the beginning, he romanced her and won her and tenderly nicknamed her Betty.

Six years later, when Joe had his new commission in the U.S. Army, he and Betty were married. Almost immediately World War I called him from his nearly completed Ph.D. program and put him on active duty. That changed their life direction, and thereafter Mother was his "lady"—through thirty-plus years in the Army and twenty-plus more years as editor-in-chief of a military publishing company.

Strong, proud, erect, everything-is-under-control Joe, who to many was Brigadier General Joseph Burton Sweet, was just "Daddy" to four of us: my older brother Bobby, me, and our two little sisters Mary Alice and Margie. We children heard him tell plenty of fun stories about his childhood—Daddy was a great storyteller. But the real truth of his bitter struggles and deprivations and childhood sufferings we had to piece together from others, even after his death.

Daddy and Mother were similar in that both were earnest, hard-driving workers; and when in their mid-thirties they accepted the Lord into their lives, that's the kind of Christians they became—true leaders who for nearly half a century taught Bible classes and tirelessly counseled and shepherded others.

But there was an unspoken sadness in their differences. Daddy was an idealist, a romantic, an irrepressible lover. He said "I love you" to Mother and Bobby and his three girls a thousand, thousand times. On the other hand, inherently shy, good, practical Mother would brush all that "silliness" away—and so her children figured "Oh, that's just Daddy," and did the same. He made us all feel very secure in our worth, but it never occurred to us to give security back to him; Daddy was Daddy. It wasn't until after his death, when we were full-blown adults, that we realized Daddy, too, was inherently shy, and he, too, had had needs. . . .

Perhaps that difference between them accounted for a lot of their frustrations and the way they often tended, in the little daily moments, to misunderstand and irritate each other.

How, then, did Joe and Betty Sweet initiate a family tree with thirty-nine descendants so far, who are all (except the littlest ones) happy, settled, productive Christians?

They were faithful to three crucial disciplines of the home:
1. They built strong habit patterns that affirmed their love for each other. They always stood up for each other with unquestioned loyalty. Their friends were all mutual friends. Their times of recreation were spent together. And after they met the Lord their life direction together became even more focused—teaching His Word and caring for those around them.

2. Together they built strong habit patterns that affirmed their love for their children. Daddy continually hugged, praised, and encouraged us; Mother exhorted and spanked; we needed both. Both parents spent time with each of the four of us. Daddy helped when we needed assistance with homework and gave us extra quarters for good grades. Mother helped with scouting and piano lessons and other extracurricular activities.

3. And together they built strong habit patterns that affirmed their love for God. Church going was as regular as breathing. Every day ended with family Bible reading and prayers. Each parent and each child knelt individually at their own bedsides for final nightly prayers. Nothing— not travel or vacations or house guests—ever altered these routines.

And daily, year after year, until their deaths, Daddy prayed out loud with Mother for every child and every grandchild by name.

The Threat

"*The only way to get this world back on track is to*
go back to the basics: how we raise our kids. . . ."
—Lee Iacocca

We've lost the world of Joe and Betty Sweet, and we can't ever get it back. "Everyone is really scared," writes Elizabeth Schorr.

She's talking about the present world's response to the thousands of kids today who are out of control—kids who've produced a labyrinthine system of cops, courts, camps, schools, foster homes, and treatment programs.

Why? These young people have learned to disdain right conduct—conduct basic to our functioning as a civilized world. Business leaders are beginning to guess that unless something changes, they could soon be faced with a "major shortage of educated, trustworthy workers."[1]

"The upheaval is evident everywhere in our culture. Babies have babies, kids refuse to grow up and leave home, affluent Yuppies prize their BMWs more than children, rich and poor children alike blot their minds with drugs."[2]

---

1. "Kids Out of Control," *Los Angeles Times*, 18 May 1989, V5.
2. Jerrold K. Footlick, "What Happened to the Family?" *Newsweek* special issue, winter/spring 1990, 16.

My own state of California has now hit all-time highs and (per capita) leads the nation in numbers of youngsters in foster care and juvenile detention.

And throughout the United States, at the beginning of the 1990s, of the nearly 63 million youngsters under eighteen, these facts are true:

- Almost a million are in foster, group, or institutional care.

- Over a million run away from home each year.

- 14 million are poor.

- Almost 10 million have no regular source of medical care.

- 20 million have never seen a dentist.

- Over two million are reported each year as suspected victims of abuse or neglect.

- Over a million are not in school.

- Each year over half a million of the girls become mothers.

- An estimated three million have a serious drinking problem.

- And the suicide rate climbs and climbs.[3]

Furthermore, say criminologists Professor and Mrs. Sheldon Glueck, "A delinquent child often grows up to produce delinquent children—not as a matter of heredity, but of his own unresolved conflicts which make him an ineffective parent." These criminologists also say they foresee no letup in this trend.[4]

"The nation's children are in trouble, and we've got to join hands and help them," says Mrs. Roseann Bentley, President

---

3. *USA Today,* 4 Oct. 1989, 11A.
4. From an interview in *U.S. News & World Report* (April 1965), and cited in *Dare to Discipline* by James Dobson (Wheaton, IL: Tyndale House—Regal Books, 1970), 92.

of the National Association of State Boards of Education. Her organization has linked up with the American Medical Association and others for one purpose—to search for ways to prevent teen drug and alcohol abuse, smoking, AIDS, and pregnancy.

She says 77 percent of U.S. teen deaths are the result of drinking and drugs. "Education alone will not change behavior. We have to involve the community."[5]

To which I say, "The community is not enough. We have to involve specifically the home—and most specifically, the Christian home."

One social worker explains the way she sees it:

> The world's complicated. Pressures on parents are increasing . . . not only for single parents who struggle to put meals on the table, but also for the Yuppie moms and dads hard pressed to make their BMW payments. . . .
>
> Parenting takes more energy than most tasks, but when parents come home drained from a day of coping with modern life, there's not much energy left for child rearing.[6]

Already, even among the offspring who seem to "succeed," we're producing a big crop of Type A's—people who are restless, anxious, time-urgent, angry, hyperaggressive, ego-driven, and basically insecure. Why are they like this? Because, say the researchers, in their formative years important people in their lives didn't care—or were perceived as not caring.

Neighborhoods, churches, schools, and families are all generally weaker than earlier in our history; values of right and wrong often aren't being taught. The result? Many children often don't "succeed" at all. And when ever-growing numbers of kids mess up, there's almost never enough system or money or personnel to salvage them.

Peter Forsythe, head of a New York foundation dealing with juvenile delinquency, says kids don't go bad the day they hit junior high:

5. *USA Today*, 20 Sept. 1989, 1A.
6. Ibid., 2A.

Parenting is a learned skill. Control starts early. If you lose it early, there's no reasserting it.

Research shows society has more luck helping bad families become functional than it does helping rotten kids become good ones. The knee-jerk reaction when a kid gets out of control is to break up the home. Got a bad kid? Send him somewhere. But that usually makes the kid worse. At a minimum, you destroy the laboratory in which the child and parents can learn to solve the problem.[7]

"The laboratory!"

Precious laboratory it is. Have you any idea how much God loves families, His own invention? How much He loves *your* family? How much He loves your kids, who are His, and how concerned He is for them?

In the very beginning of human history God established the family. In fact, three times when He's wanted to begin something special, He's started with a new family:

1. Adam and Eve and their children;

2. After the flood, Noah and his wife and children;

3. After the Tower of Babel, Abraham and Sarah and their offspring.

This third family grew to become the world's most stable social system—a system with father, family, clan, tribe, and nation.

Up the ladder, everyone was *accountable to.*

Down the ladder, everyone was *responsible for.*

Eventually, sin began to split the structure apart, from the top down. Around 600 B.C. the Hebrew nation was broken up and scattered, and with it, its tribes.

Clans went on for centuries, both Jewish and Gentile— extended families living near each other. Eventually, with increased mobility, these too were broken up and scattered.

Just since World War II, an escalation in the divorce rate has been breaking up and scattering the next rung down the ladder, the family.

---

7. Ibid., 3A.

And the status of the father is seriously eroding.

Today's world society is an impending avalanche sliding toward hell. Is your family caught in the slide? Or will you gather your loved ones and make a drastic leap to solid ground?

I said *drastic*.

Let me give you two "Drastic Don'ts" and ten "Drastic Do's"—to save you and yours out of the roaring, hell-bent avalanche that is upon us all.

After you've read them . . .

> MAKE THE RIGHT DECISIONS.
> BECAUSE THEN YOUR DECISIONS
> WILL MAKE YOU.

A drastic leap is a scary thing.

To jump all the way clear of a cascading avalanche—with the fear you'd feel, and the sheer effort of it—would be a leap you'd never forget.

If any part of your family is very close to this world's avalanche, reshaping your family at this point might well be a scary, drastic leap.

But, come to think of it, not jumping would be scarier. . . .

So let me spell out, under God's direction, what your "leap" might involve—how your family life could be reshaped to get it to the solid ground of godliness, settledness, and security.

First . . .

TWO DRASTIC DON'TS

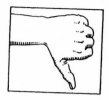

Don't Retreat

Don't try to go back to yesterday; go back to the Bible

"May you have warmth in your igloo, oil in your lamp, and peace in your heart."

—Eskimo benediction

PORTRAIT:
WALT AND SHERRY

Sherry, our firstborn, and her husband Walt Harrah (it rhymes with "Sarah") aren't your typical baby boomers—they lead the pack. They're not even today's pacesetters—they're *tomorrow's* pacesetters.

Walt's hair is shingled close up the sides and back, and the top he mousses and then scrunches into curls with his fingers. (He's also the comedian of our clan.) Sherry wears earrings that either cover most of her ears or dangle to her shoulders. Of course they drive a van. Their home's decor, where they entertain constantly, is art-deco-mod in black, white, mauve, and lavender. They've decorated it themselves, and it looks great.

Mindy, seventeen, tints her red hair a different red and likes to sing Christian rock—really well. Beth Anne, eleven, is a teenie bopper with braces, ponytail, and flouncy skirts. Andrew, five, is into Little League T-ball.

These people give up saying "cool" or "rad" almost before it starts.

And what's their passion? Jesus Christ. Walt sings and writes and produces Christian music. He leads worship at their church. He and Sherry, side by side, co-teach a large Sunday school class of young marrieds. Sherry teaches other Bible classes as well and speaks at women's retreats. Together they pour their lives and God's Word into all the others they can touch. Grandparents Joe and Betty Sweet would be proud—although, superficially, not just a little shocked.

Their uninhibited enthusiasm for following God has cost them. Even in Walt's seminary-student years, he painted houses and sang and put himself through school without Sherry's having to leave caring for home and baby Mindy. After graduation, in the years of struggle to get established freelancing in Christian music, Walt continued never to pressure Sherry to work outside the home. The cost has been great—especially in pricey Orange County —but the financial loss can't be compared to their deep satisfactions, their secure kids, and the influence of their lives on others.

What does the Bible have to say about the Harrah family's lifestyle? It certainly doesn't say women can't work. Lydia was a dealer in expensive purple fabric (Acts 16:14). Aquila and Priscilla were a married couple in business together (Acts 18:3). Dorcas was a dressmaker—although maybe not for salary (Acts 9:36, 39). The woman of Proverbs 31 bought and sold property and clothing and who knows what else (verses 13–27).

But the Bible has everything to say about seeking first God's kingdom. It has strong words about not letting concern for food and clothes get in the way of following His principles (Matt. 6:25–33).

Walt and Sherry are enthusiasts for God and for His Word. Whatever it costs doesn't matter. Their eyes are on Him, on His plans for their lives, and on the jolly good fun of carrying out those plans—hairdo's, outrageous earrings, T-ball, laughter, mauve and lavender, and all.

Henry Ford once said,

> You can do anything if you have enthusiasm. Enthusiasm is the yeast that makes your hopes rise to the stars. Enthusiasm is the sparkle in your eyes, the swing in your gait, the grip of your hand, the irresistible surge of will and energy to execute your ideas.
>
> Enthusiasts are fighters. They have fortitude. They have staying qualities. Enthusiasm is at the bottom of all progress. With it, there is accomplishment. Without it, there are only alibis.

Enthusiasts *are fighters.* They don't let their family life just go with the flow and surrender to the avalanche.

Enthusiasts *have fortitude.* They're willing to be separate from all that is cheap, vulgar, desensitizing, degrading.

Enthusiasts *have staying power.* They maintain godly habits which, over the long haul, build them into winners.

As we say, there's no return to Joe and Betty Sweet's pre-avalanche day. The way is permanently barricaded. The old line "When *I* was your age . . ." has always been obnoxious and it still is. Parent, you are out of an earlier world, and God wants you to prepare your children for still a different world to come, where you and I can't follow. But in the meantime, God's name is "I AM"! He is always "now," always relevant, always contemporary.

Enthusiasts for God and His Word are contemporary, too—though not necessarily like the Harrahs in style. But they don't occupy themselves with trying to maintain the trappings of "the good old days"—they're occupied with truth. And truth, when it is loved and sought after, has a way of transforming life from timidity and over-conservatism to reckless, radiant, radical obedience.

So here's the first Drastic Don't: *Don't try to shape your family to some former day. Don't go back to yesterday; go back to the Bible instead.* Go back to its strong, clear, makes-sense, ever-relevant teachings. Whatever is happening around you, go back to what God Himself tells you to do in His Word.

If you don't obey Him, your family can't win. If you obey Him, you can't lose.

As God helps me, I want to spell out eleven more *disciplines of the home* for the 1990s and beyond—this unprecedented era into which we've now come.

If you decide these disciplines are unbiblical, trash the book (Acts 17:11). But if you see that they square with the Word of God, then note how your family matches up with His truths.

And be prepared to make some important, thrilling changes. Get ready, under His direction and by His Spirit, before it's too late, to reshape the structure and focus and spirit of your family life.

Don't Divorce

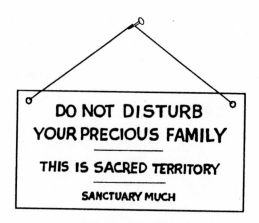

DO NOT DISTURB
YOUR PRECIOUS FAMILY

THIS IS SACRED TERRITORY

SANCTUARY MUCH

"For this reason," said God when He made Adam and Eve, "a man will leave his father and mother and be united to his wife, and they will become one flesh" (Gen. 2:24).

The two marriage partners are one whether they produce many children or none at all. Children must always be on the periphery—loved, but periphery. The man and woman are the center. When the children leave they drop off the outside, and the center remains the same.

That's the precious focal point to be guarded and protected! That's the priceless centerpiece, which is the stability of society present and future.

Some insights on Aquila and Priscilla were gleaned from a sermon I heard by Dr. Samuel Kamelesian at Ilo Ilo, Philippines, March 6, 1984.

```
┌─────────────────────────────────────────┐
│              PORTRAIT:                    │
│         A CHILDLESS MARRIAGE              │
└─────────────────────────────────────────┘
```

Did Aquila and Priscilla ever have children? Not that we know of.

When the Apostle Paul first met them they were a couple in trauma. They were displaced persons, newly arrived in Greece after having been kicked out of Rome for being Jewish. In Corinth they set up business together as tentmakers. "Paul went to see them, and because he was a tentmaker as they were, he stayed and worked with them" (Acts 18:3).

For at least a year and a half Aquila and Priscilla listened to Paul's teaching, and it so grabbed their hearts that when he moved, they moved with him. From here on they're business partners second, and bright, enthusiastic Christians first. And best friends with Paul.

What a model for a childless couple! They're never separated from each other. They give themselves tirelessly, even risking their lives (Rom. 16:4). They open up their home—to teach the great Apollos (Acts 18:26) and to house a local church (1 Cor. 16:19). In four out of six references Priscilla is named first—here we have "Mrs. and Mr."! Priscilla was obviously enormously gifted. How can a man live in the shadow of someone like that?

I see three things about this couple that answer that question.

1. They were individually liberated by faith in Christ. Priscilla had dignity given her by Him. And Aquila also was a child of God, and because of this they liberated each other. They weren't threatened. They didn't bind each other. If theirs hadn't been a secure marriage, do you think Aquila would ever have allowed famous, charismatic Apollos to come live in their house with them? No way.

2. Together, love and discipline made them a liberated unit. Their life was one. Whatever they went through, they

went through together. They rolled with the punches. Not "tit for tat" or "if you get me, I'll get you." They supported and complemented each other.

3. Together, they were free to liberate other people. Ministry was their joy. There was no sense of their criticizing Apollos; it seemed to be, "Brother, we have an extra room; would you like to stay with us?"

This was risky: Apollos would see them up close. Well, that's exactly what they had in mind! There are so many young Christians who would love to watch this kind of model couple up close. Discipling means proximity and exposure.

That's the reason why I'm including lots of stories of couples, parents, and families in this book as models. Good relationships and enthusiasm for God spawn more good relationships and enthusiasm for God.

PORTRAIT:
THE GOLDEN YEARS
OF MARRIAGE

Abram and Sarai were married before their story ever begins in Genesis 11. You just can't imagine them apart. Sarai couldn't get pregnant, either—for much of their married life—and, like Priscilla, she simply gave herself to being a loyal, faithful wife. First Peter 3 calls her a "holy woman" who was "beautiful" because she "obeyed Abraham and called him her master" (v. 6).

But Abram did some horrible things; why should she obey him? When he took her to live in Egypt he got nervous over her gorgeous good looks, for fear the Pharaoh of the land would kill him to take her for himself. So he said, "Tell everybody you're my sister." (Even good men, in times of panic, can temporarily turn into wimps.)

Sarai "obeyed Abraham." She held her head up. She did what was asked of her. And she kept in her heart her loyalty to her husband—even, indeed, in Pharaoh's palace, until the trauma was over and she was returned. *With,* add the

Scriptures, "sheep and cattle, male and female donkeys, menservants, maidservants and camels"—all donated by an embarrassed Pharaoh. Not bad Egyptian souvenirs when you've been abroad on a trip!

Years pass. Their green years turn golden. Abram grows in stature, wealth, godliness. A good woman makes a good man better. She's got to be proud and happy: he loves her, he lives with her.

Then together they're rewarded with changed names. The Lord God Almighty appears and says to Abram, "No longer will you be called Abram [Exalted Father]; your name will be Abraham [Father of Multitudes]!" (Gen. 17:5).

What's the difference? Just one sound: the letter "H"— the sound of breath. God breathes into Abram's name: "Your name will be Abrah-h-h-ham."

A marvel! God had long ago breathed into Adam, and he became a living person (Gen. 2:7). Years later Jesus would breathe His Holy Spirit into His disciples (John 20:22). (Both the Hebrew and Greek words for "breath" and "spirit" are the same.)

God breathes into Sarai's name as well. He says to Abraham, "You are no longer to call her Sarai; her name will be Sarah-h-h-h."

An exquisite reward, a spiritual high point, a new beginning in their together-life. Everything should be coming up roses from here on, right? Wrong.

They move to Gerar, Sarah is still beautiful, Abraham eyes the king, and he says, "Say you're my sister."

Abraham!! You did that one years ago! Are you really basically just a wimp, and your good actions have just been flukes? To save his own skin he puts his precious Sarah out to be vulnerable a second time—all these years later when he's supposed to be "mature." And, sure enough, she's still so beautiful, she ends up in the palace of another king.

This sort of thing brings many golden-years marriages to divorce. They've had wonderful days together and stacked up countless memories. . . . Then at midlife, that fascinating-or-fearful time which is moving inevitably toward old age, the husband may panic. He sees quietly shutting doors. He feels the terror of all those possibilities slowly closing away from view.

One way or another he becomes a fool, and off goes his wife to a lawyer.

Not Sarah! She sees the crisis come, pass, and fade, and she remains loyal. That's what makes her a winner, a "holy woman." At one point God says to Abraham, "Listen to whatever Sarah tells you" (Gen. 21:12). Beautiful.

And Sarah watches God keep fulfilling the blessings of their married love and the blessings of their shared devotion to Him. And then—He gives them a miracle baby son.

```
┌─────────────────────────────┐
│          PORTRAIT:          │
│       THE GREEN YEARS       │
│         OF MARRIAGE         │
└─────────────────────────────┘
```

Isaac was the son: the sheltered, protected, rich man's only son—and at forty he was still a bachelor. Well, why wouldn't those very old parents dote on him and cherish him? They probably had trouble even *thinking* about sharing him with a daughter-in-law.

Probably Sarah was actually the hold-out. When she finally breathed her last, then Abraham arranged for his son to get a proper wife.

This wife was Isaac's distant cousin Rebekah, whose father Bethuel seems to have been a wimp. (Notice in Genesis 24 who the family spokesman was, who made the decisions, and who got all the gifts and attention. Never Bethuel!) And because Bethuel had trouble being assertive and decisive, Rebekah's mother and brother Laban had learned, if necessary through politicking and deception, to overlook him and run the family affairs.

Isaac, somewhat of a wimp himself, is paired with Rebekah, who has grown up learning how you get around wimps. Was it God's will? Absolutely! God was looking down time's vast corridors at the race He was building and the Savior He was preparing:

"From the rocky peaks I see them,
   from the heights I view them. . . .
Who can count the dust of Jacob
   or number the fourth part of Israel? . . ." (Num. 23:9,
      10).
"Like valleys they spread out,
   like gardens beside a river,
like aloes planted by the Lord . . ." (Num. 24:6).

"I see him, but not now;
   I behold him, but not near.
A star will come out of Jacob;
   a scepter will rise out of Israel" (Num. 24:17).

But in the short view of things, here are Isaac and Rebekah, two love birds thrown together in marriage. Will
they "live happily ever after"? Not on your life.
   Rebekah can't get pregnant (shades of Sarah). Probably
they bicker and blame each other. Finally she does, and she
hates the pregnancy—I'm feeling this baby kick so much, I
must be black and blue inside. Isaac, don't just stand there,
do something.
   It's twin boys, no wonder. Oi vey. Isaac likes Esau, Rebekah likes Jacob. They polarize. Papa champions the first-
born; Rebekah shows him, she teaches her underdog twin
to con away the birthright.
   Is it possible that two people can truly fall in love, and
then totally fall out of love again? Of course. Rebekah free-
falls down so far out of love that at one point she says, "I'm
disgusted with living" (Gen. 27:46).

The green years. For one couple they withered: for Isaac
and Rebekah. Isaac could have put her away, as divorced.
He never did. They lived together; they produced the son
whose name became Israel, patriarch of the nation; and
when they died they were buried together; you can see their
tomb in Hebron to this day. And they are a mighty link in
the miracle-continuum of God's eternal promises to Abraham and to his seed.
   Looking back, they've got to be glad they stuck it out.

*   *   *   *   *

Marriage has to be an unconditional commitment to an imperfect person.

That sounds really heavy, doesn't it! What if . . . ? What if this person to whom you've promised your commitment turns out to be more imperfect than you bargained for? Let me quote from Ray's and my book *You Don't Have to Quit:*

> As God looks down on the total human scene, He sees each individual, of course. . . . But He sees more. He also sees the whole human picture; He sees the connections, the mergings together, the patterns and the oneness of the generations that . . . we can barely envision. Without the limits of time . . . God sees how you belong to your great-grandfather and how you affect your great-grandson and how, in every particular detail, you are part of the continuum of the human generations. . . .
>
> God gives hints [in His Word] of a commingling together of the behavior of generations which is unthinkable to us little people with limited perception. . . . You and we are holding hands with a great host of unseen persons in unbroken chains.
>
> What happens when you freak out and say, "Oh, heck, I quit"?
>
> When you kick over the traces?
>
> When you flee, when you say "I've had it," when you give up?
>
> What damage is that doing to the others—the whole chain of your ancestors and your descendants? What kind of permanent wound or scar are you making? What instability are you building into the line? How many will grieve? How many will be hurt? . . .
>
> Ask God for staying power, for determination, for patience, for gutsy courage to survive and survive well. . . . Your fortitude could have larger ramifications than you now know.[1]

What is God's great reason for wanting marriages to stay together?

---

1. You may also want to read all of chapter 17 in *You Don't Have to Quit,* formerly published under the title *Staying Power* (Nashville: Thomas Nelson, 1986, 1988), 102–104.

Has not the Lord made [marriage partners] one? In flesh
and spirit they are his. And why one? Because he was seeking godly offspring. (Mal. 2:15)

It's the kids He's concerned about. They affect all His future people. And He yearns for each new generation to
succeed—to be brought back into His love forever.

At last we have statistics to discover what God has known
through the millennia: *divorce ruins too many kids.* No wonder, then, He says He hates divorce (Mal. 2:16).

Divorce is hell. Divorced people everywhere are
lamenting their plight—on call-in radio, on "Oprah" and
"Donahue." Magazines are rife with stories of latchkey
kids, custody kidnappings, delinquent dads, single moms,
and offspring in shelters for the homeless.[2]

It's only recently that we've begun to realize the dam-
ages. We've thought, "Kids are resilient; they're more mature than we give them credit for," or "It's tough for now, but
eventually they'll be fine," or "Better they have one parent
with peace than two with constant arguments."

A while back a daily radio talk show psychologist spent
one week interviewing adults thirty and older whose parents had divorced years before, when they were children.

He found not one happily married. Either they had never
married at all or they'd had a series of failed marriages—
and the same reason came through over and over: they
didn't have the courage to develop a close, trusting relationship with anyone for fear of being abandoned again.

This is not to say if you're the offspring of a divorce, or
if you're raising the offsprings of divorce, that God can't
give you the miracle of healed deficiencies; "Nothing is impossible with God" (Luke 1:37). This is to say, for the sake
of those precious kids of yours or your spouse's, don't divorce any more in the future—presuming on God for another miracle; don't tempt Him!

---

2. Diane Medved, *The Case against Divorce* (New York: Donald I. Fine, 1989).

First Corinthians 7:12–14 says that the salvaging of a marriage, even an "unyoked" marriage, is what makes the children turn out not bad but good.

Writes Elizabeth Achtemeier in her book *The Committed Marriage,*

> I grew up in a home which, for a period, was marked by violent differences, arguments, and the threat of divorce. Through all the turbulence and heartache, my Christian mother refused to agree to the separation because she thought it was wrong for a Christian to do so.
>
> Some outside the family thought she was foolish, but personally I am deeply grateful to her. Contrary to the belief of some psychologists, she prevented psychic damage to her children far beyond what measure of it we suffered in a troubled home.
>
> She lived to enjoy a mellowed and loving relationship with Dad in their later years. He himself came to a simple but deep Christian faith, and the last words I heard Mother say to him before her death were, "You really love me, don't you?"[3]

If Elizabeth's mother hadn't stuck out that marriage, I wonder how Elizabeth would have turned out. I wonder if the world would ever have been blessed and helped by her wonderful book.

> All the flowers of all the tomorrows
> are in the seeds of today.

But what if you've already done it—you're divorced from previous marriages? Have you sufficiently grieved, mourned, repented?

Let me tell you what I mean with an illustration from the days of Nehemiah.

Backslidden Jews wept when they listened to the reading of God's Word. So Nehemiah said, in effect, "Buck up! This is your new-beginning time! Let the joy of the Lord be your strength." So the people dried their tears, and because it

---

3. Elizabeth Achtemeir, *The Committed Marriage* (Philadelphia: Westminster Press, 1976), 127.

was that time of year, they celebrated the happy, week-long Feast of Tabernacles.

But for them it was like dabbling in superficial ocean waves of fun when underneath, an undertow of unfinished mourning was dragging their spirits the other way. So as soon as they were left to themselves, they all gathered for a public confession, weeping, fasting, and writing down a list of new resolutions to which they all signed their names (Neh. 8–10). Only then was the old chapter truly closed, and they could follow with a genuine, powerful celebration (Neh. 12).

Said someone:

> When my dog died I was inconsolable. Finally I realized I hadn't grieved adequately when my father died when I was nine. And I'd lived all those years with a low-grade depression.

Have you sufficiently grieved and repented over previous marriage failures? Maybe you and your present partner should do it together. Schedule a time. Talk it out. Read the Bible together, perhaps Colossians 3:1–19. Pray together, out loud.

Then perhaps you need to say to each other and before God, with all your children as witnesses, "We promise never to divorce again." And celebrate it with punch and cookies!

Of course you'll still have bad times ahead. But understand that you're now committed to one another "for better or for worse, in sickness and in health, for as long as you both shall live."

Commitment means a willingness to sometimes be unhappy.

Remember what the angel of the Lord told Hagar when she ran away from home? "Return . . . and submit" (Gen. 16:9). Or think about the Apostle John. Did he feel stuck when he was exiled to the island of Patmos for life? Certainly he did. But *on that island,* not elsewhere, God met him and gave him the Book of Revelation!

> "The best way out
> is *through.*"
> —Robert Frost

NOW WORK INTO YOUR LIFE
WHAT YOU'VE BEEN READING.

Make a list of the sentences in this chapter that grabbed you, and write down why. Or in a group, take some silent time to write them down, and then read them and explain why.

For instance,

"The man and woman are the center of the family." If you're a single parent, or raising children not your own, think how God's Word gives exceptions to that situation to show that God can make up for atypical families.

Or *"divorce ruins too many kids"*—when your own children have divorced parents in their backgrounds. Think of God's powerful "exceptions to the rule":

1. Moses, taken from both parents: Exod. 1:22–2:10.
2. Samuel, taken from both parents: 1 Sam. 1:20–28; 2:11.
3. Esther, an orphan raised by a cousin: Est. 2:7.
4. Timothy, with an unbelieving father: Acts 16:1–3; 2 Tim. 1:5.

Can you think of others?

Or maybe this sentence grabbed you:

"Marriage has to be an unconditional commitment to an imperfect person."

Or,

"Commitment means a willingness to sometimes be unhappy."

Write down, or talk through with your group, how you can work the sentences that grabbed you into your own life. Then pray them in.

You're eyeing the avalanche, and you're eyeing the rock, the solid ground. Can you make it?

No, in your own strength you really can't.

But the Spirit of Almighty God can—within you. Then ask Him to help you, and to work strongly in each member of your family, as you consider . . .

TEN DRASTIC DO'S

If you'll make the leap, God is willing to start you in a new place.

THE FIRST DRASTIC DO
Slow Down

Do you want an elegant family life? Do you want an elegant marriage?

"Simplicity, carried to an extreme, becomes elegance."[1]
—Jon Franklin

It will call for drastic action to achieve that simplicity. Too many of us find ourselves wishing our microwaves would hurry up. Or we get impatient mixing our instant coffee! Thomas Carlyle (1795–1881) said simply, "There is nothing more terrible than activity without insight." But reversing a frantic lifestyle will call for a drastic slowdown.

Read the typical advice given these days to rectify the situation. The headline will say something like, "THREE JOBS, TWO KIDS, ONE PROBLEM: NO TIME."

Then the first paragraph describes the situation: the stress of parents' coping with work all day, then coming home tired each evening and rushing around buying groceries, cooking dinner, trying to catch up on housework, etc., with no extra time or energy for the family.

1. Reprinted with permission from the July 1988 *Reader's Digest*. From *Writing for Story* by Jon Franklin. Copyright © 1986 Jon Franklin. Reprinted with permission of Atheneum Publishers, an imprint of Macmillan Publishing Co.

Then this typical article gives "solutions." (Only every solution demands more time and energy—just what these two don't have!) Establish traditions. Once a week bake cookies together; another time play games. Play with the kids for five minutes each evening when you first get home: "Play and laughter will do wonders for your attitude."

Final paragraph: "Remember, life is for living, laughing, and loving, not for whining, worrying, and working."

Great! Let's goforit.

First night: We struggle through the door with the last traces of our strength and force a laugh: "Ha ha ha ho ho ho!"

The children don't even look up from the TV.

We try it closer and louder: "Let's play together. Ha ha ha ho ho ho!"

This doesn't work for well past the five minutes earmarked for play and laughter, but then at last they speak. Without moving their eyeballs they say, "When's dinner?"

We haven't cooked any; life is for living, laughing, and loving.

Finally we've gotten their full attention. "What-a-at?" We've made eye contact! Only the looks we're getting are something between hatred and war.

Still, we persist in the New Effort for a whole week— until there's not a clean piece of clothing in a single closet or drawer, we can't open the laundry-room door because of the dirty laundry packed behind it, and the used dishes have overflowed from kitchen to living room tables, sofas, and chairs, and we have to sit on the floor.

Then we go back to whining, worrying, and working.

* * * * *

The "successful" families today must be taking steroids. Here are excerpts from a Father's Day article I'm reading:

Donald is absolutely more than anyone could expect. He is always available for the four kids, the laundry, the groceries, the house. [Donald also works sixty hours a week as an oil company executive.]

> Two adults, two careers, and two children can some-
> times be too taxing. . . . I can bring home the bacon, and I
> can fry it in the pan.

> My wife works five days a week. I work four nights a
> week. I have complete responsibility for my two boys, ages
> 3 1/2 and 20 months, from 7 A.M. to 5 P.M. . . .[2]

So when does father sleep?

Unless you're the Bionic Man, year after year of this
could start to grind on you. "Trying to be 'Superdad' with
60-hour work weeks," says the Bureau of National Affairs
after intensive research, "creates stress and guilt."

An executive with a large labor union would confirm this.
His wife is an attorney; they have two boys, ages three and
two; and the dad spends about 70 percent of his time traveling. "Last week I was gone all week. I experience great guilt
and pain as a result of my reduced parenting role. . . . I
try to call my children once a day. When I'm away they
associate me primarily with phones and airplanes."

Dr. Kyle D. Pruett says this:

> Many [parents] are fragmented and frayed. The only
> way to avoid this is to think about it clearly: Am I willing to
> drop down a few rpms on the fast track to make a place in
> my heart for my children now when it matters?[3]

> ## PORTRAIT:
> ## A QUIET FAMILY

Our son Ray, Jr., took his wife Jani and the kids to north-
ern Scotland for four years, while Ray got his Ph.D. at the
University of Aberdeen. They were four quiet years. Would
it have been harder to live those years in America at the
same pace? I'm sure of it.

---

2. "The Involved Papa Is a Sign of Modern Times," *USA Today,* 16 June 1989.
3. "Dads Struggle to Juggle Kids and Jobs, Too," *USA Today,* 16 Jan. 1989.

(Ray, Sr., and I went with our Nels to live in Kabul,
Afghanistan, for part of Nels' second-grade year, and the
three of us played a lot more games and danced a lot more
"Looby Loo." Maybe one family solution would be to trade
jobs with somebody elsewhere for a while and get a true
break.)

Anyway, those years Eric was ages five to nine, Krista
was four to eight, Dane was three to seven, and Gavin was
their "wee Scot" born in Aberdeen, who came home to the
States when he was two.

Around the family table they memorized one verse from
each book of the Bible. And they talked about what each
book was about, and who the important people were in
each one. Their dad put big sheets of paper on rings like a
flip chart, to help remind them.

Over and over they played the Anything Game, which
meant just acting out any person, place, thing, animal,
idea—while the others guessed.

They took walks by the River Dee. They skipped stones.
They saw salmon jump.

They walked together to church, they walked to shops,
they walked! (They'd had to sell their car to make it.)

They ate not two but three meals together every day.
(The school let out all their little uniformed students to go
home for lunch.)

They had snow fights. They walked in the rain.

When the electricity went off, which happened fairly
often, they lit candles and told ghost stories. Otherwise in
the evenings either Ray or Jani read to them out loud; they
covered C. S. Lewis's *Chronicles of Narnia,* a child's version
of *Pilgrim's Progress,* many things.

Sometimes Ray, Sr., and I would go visit them on our
way to or from speaking overseas. What a delight to see
Krista and her mother preparing a tea party for the dolls
or doing each other's hair. To hear all the family sing Scot-
tish songs together. To listen to Ray practice his bagpipe.
To watch Jani and Krista dance the Highland Fling. To
walk to a nearby stable where mother and daughter rode
horses. . . .

When the children were in bed, the four of us adults would simply sit and talk, without turning on any lights, until we were talking almost in the dark. Then there was time to get beyond just what they or we were doing—to how we were feeling, thinking, dreaming.

* * * * *

"All I want when I come home from work after decisions and deadlines is a relatively quiet atmosphere," says a stressed-out thirty-six-year-old father of three. "Instead I get a harassed wife, fighting kids, and a rushed dinner because there's always a game or meeting to go to *right now.*"
Dolores Curran writes,

> If one member is under stress it affects the whole family. Familiar symptoms include a constant sense of urgency; underlying tension; a desire to escape—to one's room, workplace, away; a pervasive sense of guilt for not doing everything for all the people in one's life.
> I recall running into an acquaintance at the supermarket. Her eyes filled with tears as she confided how she had been berated by her child's scoutmaster for forgetting an important den meeting. On that day of the meeting, she had four after-school activities to which she chauffeured various children, had a sick child at home, and had unexpected house guests.[4]

Maybe the greatest gift you could give your children besides Jesus Christ would be the gift of time.
(This was seen in a church bulletin: "We thank Thee, Lord, for our instant coffee, ready-made cocoa, one-minute oatmeal, and pop-up waffles. In haste, Amen.")
Maybe if you all slowed down, a measure of this prayer by John Greenleaf Whittier would begin to come true:

> Drop Thy still dews of quietness
> Till all our strivings cease;
> Take from our souls the strain and stress,

---

4. Dolores Curran, *Stress and the Healthy Family* (New York: Harper and Row, 1985), 165.

And let our ordered lives confess
The beauty of Thy peace.

In your offsprings' memories, when their childhoods are over, it would be better than a new VCR or a new van in the garage.

Have you finally subscribed to the world's values? Is *doing* more important to you than *being?* Then you're pressured.

Is *what you're acquiring* more important to you than *what you're becoming?* Then you're pressured.

Are jobs more important to you than relationships? Then you're pressured.

Do you think busy-ness, speed, and efficiency rank near the top of the list of virtues? Then you're pressured.

And are you ambitious to expose your children to more than most kids get? You're probably pressuring them.

Do you have huge expectations for them to achieve in many areas at once? You're pressuring them.

Do you want them to do, to be marvelous extensions of yourself? You're pressuring them.

And, last, if you don't possess, deep in your soul, an assurance of God's acceptance of you and your family, and other people's acceptance of you and your family, then you're pressured and you're pressuring. Trying to justify yourselves, qualify yourselves, promote yourselves can take an awful lot of time.

But probably you won't change much—unless you get gripped by a realization of the destruction that your over-busy life is causing—to your family life, your spouse, your children, your friends, your relationship with God, your soul.

Says Steven Wright, "I think God's going to come down and pull civilization over for speeding."[5]

Family, listen: It's time to come to a screeching slow-down. It's time to make brave, radical cuts in everybody's

---

5. "Quotable Quotes," *Reader's Digest,* Sept. 1989, 34. Reprinted with permission from Steven Wright and *Reader's Digest.*

schedules. If the children are old enough, have a family pow-wow to discuss what might happen.

1. Maybe father shouldn't work for a while.
Jack MacDonald, thirty-one, is an architectural designer who's taken a break. Angie, his wife, is a financial analyst. Recently they moved from a small town in Tennessee to a Richmond suburb so she could take a job that didn't require travel.
That's when they decided that two salaries weren't worth it, when they have Drew, four and a half, and Drinda, two. Jack does the home keeping, and he takes his children for walks in the park; they play in the creek; they hunt for tadpoles. When the time is right, Jack says some day he'll get a master's degree and go back to work.[6]
2. Maybe mother shouldn't work for a while.

> Better a meal with vegetables where there is love than a fattened calf with hatred. (Prov. 15:17)

Good Housekeeping magazine is launching a major campaign to promote the "New Traditionalist," saying she represents "the biggest social movement since the 1960s." They say their research is showing that many women may want a side job for earning a little extra, but there's a new desire these days to bypass the all-encompassing career and focus more on home, husband, and children—to "eliminate and concentrate"!
Is it a true trend? "You're going to see more 'cashing out' as men and women exchange high-paid jobs for lower-pressure, family-oriented lifestyles," says Faith Popcorn of Brain-Reserve.[7]
Now there's a support group called "Mothers at Home" that has seen its membership mushroom from 648 members in 1984 to 8,000 in 1989 and a magazine called *Welcome Home*—"a publication in support of mothers who choose to stay at home."

---

6. "Staying at Home Is a Full-Time Job," *USA Today,* 16 June 1989.
7. "Return to Tradition?" *Los Angeles Times,* 26 Dec. 1988, 1V.

3. *Maybe the teenage children shouldn't work yet.*
We laud their ambition; maybe our values are upside down. Should they be ambitious for more time, rather than for more money? Are their jobs draining their energies from their intellectual and spiritual preparations for life? "How much better to get wisdom than gold, to choose understanding rather than silver!" (Prov. 16:16).

4. *Maybe everybody needs to cut down, for now, on classes, projects, involvements.*
You probably can make do with less money, but you definitely need more time and exposure to each other.

These family years of yours are so precious, and they can never be reclaimed. Only *now* is when your children are being formed. There are no reruns, no instant replays. This is all you get.

A hardware store in Vashon, Washington, has a blackboard sign headed "Today's Special." For years, the chalked-on message has never been other than "So's tomorrow."

* * * * *

SLOW DOWN FOR AN ELEGANT MARRIAGE
"Never yell at each other unless the house is on fire."

The home isn't only for the children, it's also for the grownups. If there are only two of you without children, or if there are still two of you with children (whether you're parents or step-parents)—you're both responsible to set the pace and the tone of your family life.

You need to be there for each other.

You need to check each other occasionally: "Are you in accord with me, as I am with you?" (2 Kings 10:15).

You need time together, small talk, consideration of one another.

You need, husband and wife, drastic new exposures to each other. With a true pioneering spirit that's excited, cautious, relentless, you need to push into each other's hearts where no one else has ever been before, and discover, all on your own, what has never before been fathomed in your partner by anyone but God: the dark places, the bright places, the agonies and the ecstasies. And the more you come upon, the more you gather it all up in your arms and say, "This is all mine, God's gift to me," and hold tightly this amazing, labyrinthine, dearest treasure who is your Other Self.

Are there things in your partner you don't like? Well, there are things in *yourself* you don't like. Your partner has to take those as part of the whole love-package, so you take your partner's as well.

PORTRAIT:
THE JENSENS

Roger and Mary Jensen, fifty-one and forty-five, have come successfully into the middle years of marriage. Roger is six feet five and "190 pounds of smooth, coordinated muscle"—but then, I'm quoting him! He's had seventeen years of coaching high school varsity basketball and tennis, followed by seven more in public school administration. Mary is also tall, and exquisitely lovely. She used to teach P.E., too, but she's been a housewife since the children: six-foot-five Jeep, nineteen and on a college basketball scholarship; Jimmy, fourteen; and Jodi, thirteen.

This family looks like Successful America, but it has weathered two total traumas:

One, a terrible car accident which hurt them all but nearly took Jimmy's life. After his week in a coma and many months of slow recuperation, Jimmy was in "special ed" classes because of learning disabilities, but now he's back in regular classes again. He's got a supportive family, and Jimmy's a fighter.

Two (and Roger and Mary consider this one far more traumatic), their sixth and seventh years of marriage, when they became "deeply disenchanted" with each other. They wanted to divorce. They felt stuck.

Both of them took time. Instead of making a hasty decision which would have blown apart everything, separately they waited on the Lord. They cried to Him.

Says Mary, "We both went harder than ever after the Lord, and then He brought us back again to each other."

Says Roger, "I decided that I was going to treat Mary with the kindness of Christ because *He* deserved it, she didn't."

Echoes Mary, "I remember ironing Roger's shirt and praying, 'Lord, I can't stand him, but I iron this shirt for You.'"

Both hung in with their godly habits of many years, their prayer lives, their devotional lives. . . . They took time. They waited.

"It actually took several years," says Roger, "and it was the toughest thing either of us has ever been through. But eventually our love for each other bloomed again."

For a long time neither of them disclosed to anybody the agony they'd been through. Finally, after much hesitation, prayer, and embarrassment, they shared it with their weekly small group—their very best friends. And then the group broke open, and every other couple confessed that they were either going through the same thing or had in the past! And as a result of Roger and Mary's honest confession, several other marriages got healed.

Today they look so elegant and happy together—and ornamented by those three secure, happy young people! Mary and Roger have looked deeply into what each other truly is, and they have deliberately gathered it all up in their arms and said, "This person is all mine, God's gift to me, and I totally receive this, my life partner."

*   *   *   *   *

"Each one of you . . . must love his wife as he loves himself, and the wife must respect her husband" (Eph. 5:33). It's a command to be obeyed. It's a discipline to be accepted.

Don't be objecting, "But what if . . . ?" and start conjuring up extreme examples of someone's being married to the Devil himself. Most of us are just ordinary, self-centered, obnoxious sinners, and we marry other ordinary, self-centered, obnoxious sinners. The challenge is to "love" and "respect" *anyway*. To give each other time. To be patient. To be compassionate. To think the best, to view with hope.

To deeply study that stranger to whom God has joined you (Matt. 19:6). And to seek to understand.

You need to come to *know* each other.

"Adam knew Eve his wife, and she conceived and bore Cain," says the King James Version of Genesis 4:1. Recent translations say "Adam lay with his wife"; *The Living Bible* says "Adam had sexual intercourse with his wife." But the 1959 Berkeley Version says it like the old King James, "Adam knew his wife"—with a footnote that reads, "'Knew' is the correct translation; it suggests the most intimate relationship between man and woman."

And have you noticed 1 Peter 3:7 in the King James? It reads, "Husbands, dwell with [your wives] according to knowledge." It's a special call to every husband to become the world's foremost authority on his wife, getting to know her thoroughly, intimately, more and more; knowing secrets about her that are strictly exclusive with you; knowing, for instance, through perhaps years of trial and error, what are special ways to give her pleasure.

All this takes time. It takes more time. It takes high-priority time. It takes sacrificial time.

"Adam knew his wife. . . ."

Slow down.

Ray and I take frequent little "mini-vacations." We may be in Tiberias or Timbuktu, but for a couple of hours we quit. We take a walk. We play "Battleship" (only paper and pencils needed). We explore wherever we happen to be. We talk. We sleep!

Slow down.

You've had cups of tea on the couch in front of the fire, you've talked and cuddled and talked and fondled and talked . . . and then you know each other.

It's a holiday afternoon and the kids are at their cousins'. You've played checkers and shared some Scripture and lain on the floor with Diet Cokes and talked and stroked each other. . . . You know each other.

It's late at night but you're agitated over a problem between the two of you, and although you need sleep, you have to talk it out. Wrapped tight in each other's arms

you spell out the issue, you seek to understand, you confess, you weep, you kiss, you comfort, you know each
other.

To chronically race home from work, shove stuff into
the oven and into the clothes washer, discuss the most
pressing budget and schedule items, fall into bed for a
wordless quickie to relieve tensions, and then race back to
work again—that's grotesque. It's worse than a bad joke,
it's just a pathetic, repulsive caricature of a marriage. And
that kind of pattern results in living with a stranger,
and it's certainly not natural to love a stranger.

> Do not wear yourself out to get rich;
>   have the wisdom to show restraint. (Prov. 23:4)
>
> Why spend . . . your labor on what does not satisfy?
>   (Isa. 55:2)
>
> In vain you rise early
>   and stay up late,
> toiling for food to eat—
>   for [the Lord] grants sleep to those he loves. (Ps. 127:2)
>
> He provides food for those who fear him. (Ps. 111:5)

Give the sacrifice of time, in the home, for each other.
You'll be saying by your very presence, "You're wanted. I'm
here for you. You're my best friend! I enjoy being with you
more than with anybody. I love you."
Slow down.

In today's culture that's a "Drastic Do."

NOW WORK INTO YOUR LIFE
WHAT YOU'VE BEEN READING.

This chapter is in head-on collision with our current culture's lifestyle, isn't it! If these words seem drastic to you, determine not to form your way of life according to society around you but from the Word of God.

1. Prayerfully, thoughtfully, read and apply to your own family needs:

Psalm 23:1
Psalm 37:7; 46:10
Psalm 131
Proverbs 17:1
Isaiah 30:15
1 Thessalonians 4:11
1 Timothy 2:1–2
1 Peter 3:4
Isaiah 32:17.

2. Make a list of the ways you yourself could shift down to a more reasonable pace of life, to lead the way for your family. If in a study group, discuss these together.

3. Pray for your family members to be unified—to reach shared decisions about meaningful changes in the family pace.

4. If you're a working single parent, a family supporter with unusual medical bills, or in some other desperate situation where you see no true solution, remember Hagar! Read Gen. 21:14–20. As you look to God and trust Him, expect Him to work miracles for you. Pray together in your group for this.

Be There

"Mankind owes to the child the best it has to give."
—U.N. Declaration

A real estate broker asked a young woman if she was thinking about buying a house.

"Why would I need a house?" she answered. "I was born in a hospital, educated in a college, courted in a car, married in a church; I eat my meals in restaurants and spend my evenings at the movies. When I die I'll be buried from a mortuary.

"I don't need a house; all I need is a garage."

Oh, but a house can headquarter a home. And a home is an incubator for ideals and virtues and visions! Character craves a climate, a locale to spring from, and for that, only a home will do.

Money can build or buy or rent a house.

Add love to that and you have a home.

Add God to that and you have a temple. You have "a little colony of the Kingdom of Heaven."

A Christian home is a powerful show-and-tell. Through the years Christian homes have won more Christian converts than all preachers and teachers put together.

Writes Charles Colson,

Ordained by God as the basic unit of human organization, the family is not only necessary for propagating the race, but is the first school of human instruction. Parents take small, self-centered monsters . . . and teach them to share, to wait their turn, to respect others' property. These lessons translate into respect for others, self-restraint, obedience to law—in short, into the virtues of individual character that are vital to society's survival.[1]

Says Dr. John Perkins, who works so effectively with inner-city families, there are three basic human needs, and all three ought to be met in the home:

1. *Every human needs to be loved, to feel he belongs.* Over and over, even when your child seems most obnoxious, you need to be saying,

"Susie, I love you tons. I'm so glad you're my kid."

"Steve, I know sometimes you feel stuck with a lousy mother, but don't give up on me, and I'll never give up on you. We belong! We're both Joneses, and we're gonna hang in there together."

"Karen—'remember who loves ya, baby.'"

"Hey, Todd, we're the great Gruesome Twosome. I've got you, and you've got me."

All through the years, din those kinds of words into their ears. They must learn to understand grace: that your love for them isn't based on their works, that your acceptance of them isn't conditioned on their behavior.

And Dr. Perkins says,

2. *Every human needs his own space, a place which is no one else's, and a sense of assurance that nobody's going to take it away.*

Make sure each child has a sense of "territory," a room or part of a room where he can stake his claim, and possessions which are only his.

It can be tough. Our son Nels kept a pair of mice for a while. He had a deal with his best friend Mike who had

---

1. *Against the Night* (Ann Arbor, MI: Servant, 1989), 76–77.

a snake. Every time Nels' mice had babies, the snake had lunch.

Then Nels himself got a snake, only one spring it escaped. In the fall it came out of the heating vent into the living room, when I was entertaining ladies.

So much for the children's possessions.

And Dr. Perkins says,

3. *Every human needs to be affirmed, to be considered significant.* Tell your kids things like this all the time:

"Joey, you're going to be a winner in this world. I can see it coming. Look out, everybody—!"

"Debbie, I'm so proud of your drawing. Maybe you're going to grow up to be a wonderful artist."

"Mike, you're really smart. I think your study habits are starting to get better, and all those brains are going to pay off!"

And forever give them hugs, tweaks, lip-smacks on the cheek, pinches, love-punches, downright wrestling on the floor—whatever. It all says, "I'm aware of you, and I like you."[2]

Our wonderful Jewish neighbors are proud grandparents, with frequent pictures and reports. Stella says to me, "You know what a genius is? It's an ordinary kid with a Jewish grandmother!" It seems to me Jewish families do tend to root for each other, and maybe it's one reason why they often achieve in such extraordinary ways.

I know a son who told his dying father, "You gave me the most precious gift you could give me—the gift of delight. You've delighted in my presence and in all my doings. For all that you've done as a father I thank you; but most of all, I thank you for the gift of your delight."

On one of the first pages of His Book, our heavenly Parent assures us right away that when He made us He thought His creation was "very good." And throughout the rest of Scripture, in spite of His parental agonies over our sins, He keeps reaffirming that same delight:

---

2. See my book *Children Are Wet Cement* (Old Tappan, NJ: Revell, 1978).

The Lord takes delight in his people. (Ps. 149:4)

[The Lord] rescued me because he delighted in me.
   (Ps. 18:19)

The Lord disciplines those he loves,
   as a father the son he delights in. (Prov. 3:12)

The Lord your God is with you,
   he is mighty to save.
He will take great delight in you,
   he will quiet you with his love,
   he will rejoice over you with singing. (Zeph. 3:17)

To feel loved, to belong, to have a place, and to hear one's dignity and worth often affirmed—these are to the soul what food is to the body. And as you provide these for your youngsters, you're confirming their dignity, their worth, and their projected place of value in tomorrow's world.

These basic needs cannot be fulfilled by many of the parents today who divorce, work, travel, or who simply are too busy or too distracted—at the children's lifestage when they're most impressionable, fragile, and vulnerable. Unfortunately, the substitutes for meeting these three needs are everywhere: alcohol, drugs, and illicit sex. So misery abounds, abortions multiply, and prisons overflow.

However you can manage it, *be there!* Be available in your home for all the children-years. And deliberately seek to meet these three basic needs, by words and actions, as fully as you can.

But you're saying, "Look, I have to face the practical realities of living in this world. This seems too drastic to be taken totally seriously!"

But you live in a time of drastic wickedness and danger, and to go against the trends means accepting drastic solutions.

Parent-child love itself should be passionate, ultimate, drastic: "If you take [him] from me . . . you will bring [me] down to the grave in misery" (Gen. 44:29).

It's how your heavenly Parent loves:

"How can I give you up, Ephraim?
How can I hand you over, Israel?" (Hos. 11:8)

"While [the prodigal son] was still a long way off, the
father saw him and was filled with compassion for him; he
ran to his son, threw his arms around him and kissed him"
(Luke 15:20).

The kids must know! They must hear loud and clear how
loved and wanted they are in this world! What more powerful way can they learn this than for you to be saying by your
very presence, "You're wanted. I'm here for you. I like to be
with you. I enjoy you. I delight in you! I'm available."

*The average American mother spends eleven minutes a day
in focused conversation with her children—the average father,
only eight minutes!*[3] Can you imagine the damage that's doing to our children?

Says Dr. William Koch, child and adolescent psychiatrist
at Lenox Hill Hospital in New York, "You teach a child to be
charitable, first of all, by giving enough of yourself to the
child. If the child feels that he has enough, then he's able
to give."[4]

Sherry and Margie were both born in the wintertime,
which meant they could have started into kindergarten before the age of five and into first grade before six. But we
chose to keep them home for one more year of close parent-
association, and we explained often to people in their presence, "We're starting them a little late. We love having them
home; they're such a joy to us."

Says the Lord in Deuteronomy 6:6, "These command-
ments that I give you today are to be upon your hearts.
Impress them on your children. Talk about them when you
sit at home and when you walk along the road, when you lie
down and when you get up."

---

3. Blayne Cutler, *American Demographics* (Ithaca, NY), as cited in *Reader's Digest*, Sept. 1989, 189.
4. *Childlife*, autumn 1989, 5.

The making and shaping of a good human being is an awesome task.

> Every family experience determines a child's adult character, the inner picture he'll harbor of himself, how he sees others and feels about them, his concept of right and wrong, his capacity to establish warm, sustained relationships necessary to have a family of his own, his attitude toward authority and toward the Ultimate Authority in his life, and the way he attempts to make sense out of his existence. No human interaction has greater influence on his life than his family experience.[5]

PORTRAIT:
THE MARK ODUM FAMILY

I read in a magazine yesterday about Mark and Myrtle, ages thirty-four and thirty-five. Along with their five-year-old son Jared, they're a handsome black trio living in St. Louis. The three of them are practically always together, says the article, as Dad and Mom run a political consulting and public relations firm out of their home.

They make less money than if they had two incomes working separately elsewhere—but they have a lot more satisfaction, and they're financially "in the black." Besides, they say, the freedom to choose clients whose views are compatible with theirs makes up for the lower income.

"We feel better about making less money on political campaigns," says Myrtle, "than making more money by helping to promote cigarettes or liquor."

I have a picture of them here on my desk, sitting on the front porch of their eighty-year-old home. Mark's behind a table full of papers, making a call on his cellular phone. Jared is curled up on his mother's lap as she participates in the phone conversation.[6]

---

5. Armand M. Nicholi II, "The Fractured Family," *Christianity Today,* 25 May 1979, [909] 11.

6. *Business Week,* 25 Sept. 1989, 44.

```
┌─────────────────────────────────────┐
│          PORTRAIT:                    │
│      DICK AND MARY NORRIS             │
└─────────────────────────────────────┘
```

I made a long-distance call yesterday to our friend Dick Norris. Dick and Mary these days are bursting with pride and joy.

"Six kids, eleven grandchildren," said Dick. "Five have married well; they're all church leaders with Christian families. Stephen is fifteen; he's the only one left at home, and he really loves the Lord, too. His course is set."

"Dick," I said, "you have one of the most 'family' families I've ever known; the sense of Norris identity among the eight of you is so strong. Why?"

"We literally did everything together, under one roof," said Dick. "You know the business [selling cookware] was out of our home. Mary and I were both right there all the time. And as the kids began to get bigger, they all learned work, and they all helped. Vickie joined her mother doing paper work. The boys got packages ready and stacked shelves with merchandise, and when they could drive they delivered sets.

"These kids could see before their very eyes that what we all did together paid the family bills; it put bread on their own family table and bought their clothes.

"And also, it meant Mary and I were both right there teaching and living values before them."

(Two little words were running through my head: *Be there. . . ."*)

"I'm a morning person," continued Dick, "but Mary's the night owl. Just yesterday Vickie was saying how much it meant to her that during her struggles as a young person, she knew her mother was always available for the two of them to sit on stools at the kitchen counter and talk into the night."

Added Dick, "She says it was harder to talk to her dad. I'm working on that."

Midstream in their family's life, the Norrises phased out selling cookware, left heavily populated Southern

California and moved to the coast of Oregon. And what did they do there? They bought a motel, a family venture, where everyone could work together on the spot! At the time of my phone call Stephen, fifteen, was painting it. . . .

*   *   *   *   *

How can you "be there" for your family? What are the needs around you that could be met in your home—and bring you money without your leaving the kids?

Says *Business Week* Magazine, "[In the 1990s and beyond] there will be pressure on business to accommodate a little breathing space for people, especially talented ones."

It reports that already Pacific Bell, for instance, offers its 62,000 workers the option of staggered shifts. And its managers get more: if they want they can work at home by telecommuting with personal computers supplied by the company! On any given day, out of 17,000 managers a thousand may be working at home.

Or once the last child is in school full time, can you work elsewhere during school hours only?

Because Ray and I travel and minister together so constantly, there's a wonderful young woman who weekly cleans our house and feeds and waters the plants. Sometimes her thirteen-year-old son works side-by-side with her on school holidays, and he's about as good as she is! Nancy explains that he's learned because all four of them clean their own house together every week as a team: Dad, Mom, the son, and a ten-year-old daughter.

Nancy announced to me today that both children got straight A's on the past year's report cards; obviously their morale is high. And now she tells me that Russ, her husband, misses her at his present job, so he's quitting. In past years they worked together in a greenhouse nursery and then ran a small restaurant together, so now together they're going to clean houses.

That suits Ray and me fine. As far as we're concerned, all four of them can come clean our house, too—and be all together for a few more hours each week.

NOW WORK INTO YOUR LIFE
WHAT YOU'VE BEEN READING.

1. Separately or in a study group, read Deuteronomy 6:4–9. Think about how obedience to this lifestyle shaped the early Israelite families, clans, tribes, nation.

2. Read 2 Kings 11:1–3, 12, 17–21; 12:1, 2 to see the difference the priest Jehoiada made because he was willing to be a surrogate "parent" and stay close to a newborn, Joash, and protect and raise him. Because of Jehoiada's closeness to Joash, how long did the nation Israel enjoy peace and righteousness?

What might have been the difference without Jehoiada? (If you want to explore this further, see 2 Chron. 24:15 ff.)

3. Read in Proverbs 4:1–4 Solomon's description of his father David, Solomon, and Solomon's own children. Is this the pattern of your own family's generations? If not, think how the pattern could begin with you, to produce godly descendants.

In a group, describe families you know who model godliness in several generations. What do you think are some keys to their success?

4. Read Psalm 78:1–7. Pray alone or in a study group for opportunities to influence others in your family line.

Rediscover Discipline

*"If one examines the secret behind a championship
football team, a magnificent orchestra, or a successful business, the principal ingredient is invariably
discipline."*[1]

—James Dobson

I want to give you a principle for perhaps, under God,
producing the kind of children you long to produce.

> Methods are many,
> Principles are few.
> Methods always change,
> Principles never do.[2]

Our second daughter Margie and her John are enthusiasts for God. Anybody who knows them knows their fer-
vor, their delightful, contagious zeal for Him.

I remember when they'd come over to see us when their
kids were three, two, and one. John and Margie would
perch on the couch, so excited they were nearly falling off
the cushions, exclaiming, "Dad and Mom, we've just got to

---

1. James Dobson, *Dare to Discipline* (Wheaton, IL: Tyndale House—Regal
Books, 1970), 94.
2. Source unknown.

tell you everything the Lord's been doing! Listen to this, this is so tremendous you won't believe it. . . ."

And Ray and I would be smiling weakly, trying to appreciate all the wonders of God's mighty acts when out of our eyes' corners we could see one youngster drooling chocolate over the wingback, another reaching to destroy the sheet music on the piano, and the third kid lost in heavy concentration as he filled up his pants. . . .

I had lunch with Lisa, their oldest, the other day. Lisa has finished two years at Biola University. She's gorgeous, and she and a wonderful, godly young man are in love. And Lisa was leaning across the table nearly falling off her chair exclaiming to me, "Grandmother, I've just got to tell you everything the Lord's been doing! Listen to this, this is so tremendous you won't believe it. . . ."

See what I mean?

The parenting thing isn't so much "Do what I say" as it is "Be what I am" and "Do what I do." Like it or not, what you are and do will speak so loudly they can't hear what you say. They will become like you. Scary, isn't it!

Then here's an important principle you must never forget:

Successful parenting means:

One, becoming what you should be.
And two, staying close enough to the children for it to rub off.

Said Gideon, a great inspirer and motivator, "Watch me. . . . Follow my lead. . . . Do exactly as I do" (Judg. 7:17). Wrote the great Apostle Paul,

Follow our example. . . . [We] make ourselves a model for you to follow. (2 Thess. 3:7, 9)

Join with others in following my example, brothers. . . . Whatever you have learned or received or heard from me, or seen in me—put it into practice. (Phil. 3:17; 4:9)

I plead with you, brothers, become like me. (Gal. 4:12)

So first, whether there are one or two parents to do this, *become what you should be.*

There are two ways to get milk into a newborn. You can put formula into a bottle and stick the bottle in his mouth. In that case you can be there or not, go nightclubbing, eat garlic, do what you please.

Or you can breastfeed your baby, which means staying on schedule, staying rested, and eating the right things. The second way demands personal discipline, closeness, *being there.*

And when we talk about discipline in the home I don't mean first the child's; I mean your own.

> We were gentle among you [wrote Paul to the Thessalonians], like a mother caring for her little children. We loved you so much that we were delighted to share with you not only the gospel of God but our lives as well, because you had become so dear to us. (1 Thess. 2:7, 8)

Don't stick your parenting formula into a bottle and turn it over to somebody else. Give your children not only rules for living but your own lives as well, because they are dear to you.

What will you become in order that your offspring may turn out to be great human beings for God?

> When I began to tithe, I found that for several years I had to give up the purchase of an automobile. When I began starting my day with prayer, I found it meant giving up reading my morning newspaper. When I began to reach after Christian love, I found that I had to give up a multitude of prejudices against a multitude of people.[3]

You see, disciplining your children can't happen effectively until you've disciplined yourself.

"Disciplining" means channeling, focusing yourself. It means "eliminating and concentrating." A river can be spread out all over the place, sluggish and slow. It has little

---

3. Frederick M. Meek, "Christian Discipline," *The Princeton Seminary Bulletin,* (date unknown), 30.

force that way, although it can do great damage. But if you channel it, narrow it down, limit it, then you increase its drive and force, and it can power a hydroelectric plant.

That's what discipline does. "It teaches us to say 'No' to ungodliness and worldly passions, and to live self-controlled, upright and godly lives in this present age" (Titus 2:12). Restraint on the one hand. Commitment on the other. "Eliminating and concentrating!"

Discipline is for the parents first. You can't lead your children over paths you yourself haven't trod.

You say to them, "Go to bed," and you expect them to get up and go. Is God saying to you, "Go to prayer meeting"? Or, "Go to that prison ministry"?

You tell your kids to eat their food. Is God telling you to feed regularly on His Word?

You give your youngsters allowances, and you consider it your right to guide them in handling those monies. Do you let your heavenly Parent guide you in handling yours?

"Keep his decrees and commands . . . so that it may go well *with you and your children after you*" (Deut. 4:40, italics mine).

Here's the principle again:

Successful parenting means:

> *One, becoming what you should be.*
> *And two, staying close enough to the children for it to*
>   *rub off.*

"Good, the more communicated, more abundant grows," said John Milton (1608–1674). Yogi Berra said it this way: "You can observe a lot just by watching."

Step two is as crucial as step one. Stay close enough!

In you they must *see good*, over and over through the years until hopefully they've copied it.

In you, when they see bad—which they certainly will— they must also see *sorrow for the bad*, confessions, apologies, humility. Hopefully, through years of close association, they'll copy that humility, too.

But good must be good, and bad must be bad.

Our day is a growing mixture of unhealth, tolerance, lack of discernment, confusion. God says,

> Woe to those who call evil good and good evil, who put darkness for light and light for darkness. (Isa. 5:20)

And He tells us,

> Hate what is evil; cling to what is good. (Rom. 12:9)

This sounds so easy, so black and white. But it's tough, isn't it! It's hard to know what sins are bad enough to be worth "blood." In the battle against your kids' waywardness, you can't die on every hill. The big question is when to be tough? When to be tender?

> George Washington's father: "George, did you chop down the cherry tree?"
> George: "Yes, father, I cannot tell a lie. I did it with my little hatchet."
> George's father gives George a big hug.
> George's father to George's brother: "Did you push over the outhouse?"
> George's brother: "Yes, father, I cannot tell a lie. I did it with one big push."
> George's father gives George's brother a thrashing.
> George's brother: "Father! Why did you do that? When George confessed he chopped down the cherry tree, you gave him a hug!"
> George's father: "I wasn't sitting in the cherry tree."

As I say, it's hard for fallible parents to figure out how to discipline with true justice. Sometimes any words at all are almost too much. I love Ring Lardner's line, "'Shut up,' he explained."

But why does God say "hate evil, cling to good"? Because "sin, when it is full-grown, gives birth to death" (James 1:15). You don't kiss and hug somebody who has smallpox. Sin is destructive, powerful, terrifying.

So when we reach out to touch it—God says, "Whom I love [whom I really care about and want to have the happiest possible life] I rebuke and discipline" (Rev. 3:19). He disciplines us because He loves us so much—and more: it's how He proves we're really His children.

If your neighbor's kid has bad manners at your table, you don't correct him. On the other hand, your very correction of Junior proves he's yours, and you care about his behavior and you're responsible for it.

Then,

> Endure hardship as discipline; God is treating you as sons. . . . If you are not disciplined . . . then you are illegitimate children and not true sons. (Heb. 12:7, 8)

And Hebrews 12 here infers that discipline is basically to occur between parents and their children ("fathers" and "sons"), not between child-tenders and their charges. Why? Because the parents alone are responsible to God for their children's behavior, and their standards of behavior are unique. Before Him, they don't answer to anybody else's standards of behavior.

And the pattern starts with the parents first: As you submit to the discipline of your heavenly Parent, you have every right to expect that your own children will submit to yours.

When they don't? Then sin and pain must early be linked together in their minds. During the two's and following, if "no no" is deliberately ignored, a short, quick spanking comes. (Is there anything else as immediate and as eloquent?) When they knowingly, willfully sin, then there must be pain—your pain, of course, but theirs, too. Punishing is the deliberate infliction of hurt.

Of course we're not talking about child abuse. Still, it's crucially important that children grow up convinced that sin and hurt go together. That's how they learn to fear and hate sin!

But when they submit? Reward them lavishly; commend them, make over them! When children learn that good and pleasure go together, that's how they learn to go after the good.

Our heavenly Parent said it first: "Hate what is evil; cling to what is good" (Rom. 12:9).

And I mean, really openly commend them and make over them and enjoy them! If during their preschool years you were faithfully linking their disobediences with pain and their obediences with pleasure and fun and good things— you'll have started to win the battle.

Sin, thanks to the "old nature," will always be there, as it is with you and me—but it will be the unusual, the aberration. The direction of their life will be toward obedience— which means, turn on the charm and make their childhood fun! They're beginning to learn that the righteous life is the good life!

PORTRAIT:
THE McCLURES

Daughter Margie McClure said to me today, "Somehow, parents need permission to brag about their kids. They need to know that if their youngsters are basically, generally, on track, it's okay to be wildly enthusiastic about them!"

John and Margie are wildly enthusiastic about their kids.

It's football season now—and their Bud is playing for his high school with all his heart. At the game last Friday night I counted twelve of us there just to root for Bud: his four grandparents, his parents, his sisters Lisa and Laurie with their boyfriends, and his Uncle Nels with his girlfriend.

And did we hoot and holler for him—especially Friday because it was Bud's seventeenth birthday. He got the works! We had a huge paper banner with "HAPPY BIRTHDAY JOHN McCLURE" for the whole stadium to read. Even his teachers teased him about it on Monday and asked, "Who were all those people?"

"Oh, just my family," said Bud, embarrassed but proud. (We take every chance we can in the family to say "That's our boy" or "That's our girl.")

After the game of course we all charged down onto the field with our banner wildly flopping, and Bud kissed every one of us—me, twice, I think by mistake.

Bud is a kisser. Everybody kisses everybody in our family. It's what you do to say hello or goodbye.

Let me illustrate. Last year Bud worked as a towel man at the athletic club in town where Ray, his grandfather, is a member and works out. Like any typical athletic club, most of its members are macho, body-conscious, egocentric, foul-mouthed, and "cool"—above all, you gotta be cool.

Picture this, then: Ray comes into the club, spots Bud across the way, and calls out "Hey, Buddy!" Bud drops everything and rushes over for bearhugs. And a bunch of cool cats act as if it's "unreal"—but they look a little wistful.

Or one more picture. Big, tough, modest, nice, kinda-bashful Bud frequently brings a bunch of his big, tough, nice friends to his house, just hanging around. Then they'll all decide to go out—so Bud kisses his mom and dad and goes.

The guys pick up on it. Not a word . . . no kidding about it, no goofing around . . . but the last few months when they go out they all kiss Bud's mom goodbye. It's what you're supposed to do at the McClures' house.

Last week was especially touching. One of the fellows has a rather harsh, difficult father. The "swarm" is heading out; Bud kisses his dad goodbye, and the friend kisses Bud's dad goodbye, too.

*   *   *   *   *

So here's the principle once more.

Successful parenting means:

One, becoming what you should be.
And two, staying close enough to the children for it to
   rub off.

We went to a wedding Saturday. Along the way in the ceremony the bride and groom lighted a "unity candle." Separately, they each took a candle burning alone, and then together, they held the two candles close to the third candle. And neither of them moved away until they were sure that the third candle had "caught," that it was burning, too, that it was producing a flame all on its own.

Remember—when the parents are becoming what God wants them to be, and the parents and children are spending a lot of time in their house together being family, then the house becomes a home, and the home becomes an incubator for ideals, virtues, and visions.

It's the way the fire is "caught."

PORTRAIT:
MYRON AND GALE SALISIAN

Our friend Myron Salisian is tall, dark, and enthusiastic. He's a forty-five-year-old Armenian American, married to tiny, blond Gale. Their children are Matt, ten, and Robin, seven.

Matt and Robin are real kids; they can make faces and punch each other like any kids if the occasion demands. But your overriding impression of them—and it's the obvious, correct impression—is that they're secure, obedient, happy kids.

Last night over spaghetti for the six of us, Ray and I asked how come.

Myron said, "When these kids of ours arrived, Gale and I were committed to making them our number-one project, seriously giving them our time. From their births on to this day, they get about two and a half hours of both of us each evening, from dinner until their bedtimes, in addition to other times of the day."

"What happens during those two and a half hours?" we asked.

"About four in the afternoon I phone Gale, and we talk fifteen or twenty minutes if we need to. That's so when I get home we won't be bursting with things to tell each other, but we can give ourselves fully to the kids.

"Then the time includes dinner, family devotions, games, stories, winding down, and tucking into bed."

"Baths?" I asked.

"Earlier we bathed them and stayed with them while they played a little in the water. Now, of course, for that they're on their own."

"How long does tucking into bed take?" I asked.

"Oh, about an hour," said Gale. "Our kids both take a long time to relax and go to sleep. Myron spends almost all of that time with Matt, and I'm with Robin. At the very end we switch just to give goodnight hugs and kisses."

"Has this routine meant very much sacrificing of other things?" we asked.

"Oh, yes," said Myron. "The first few years it meant no community service (I knew I'd have the rest of my life to make that up) and saying no to a lot of extra church activities as well."

"But being together as a family more than made up for all that, right?"

"Oh, come on, gimme a break," they said. "Most nights got pretty routine. I mean, how challenging is it for a six-foot, forty-year-old man to play games with toddlers? And sometimes at the end of the day, we were just plain tired, and/or more eager to be with each other."

Gale said, "Sometimes we'd look at each other at dinner and sing 'It's a long time to "nighty, darling"—you know, to the tune of 'It's a Long Road to Tipperary.' 'Nighty darling' was kind of our sign-off expression with the kids. . . . No—one-, two-, and three-year-olds aren't usually all that thrilling.

"Of course now," she added, "at ten and seven they've come into the fun years. It seems as if the more their minds and personalities develop, the more we really enjoy them."

A year ago this January, Ray and I took Myron and Gale as our team when we ministered to missionaries in Italy. Myron had been overseas only once and Gale, not for fifteen years. And they'd never been two weeks away from the children.

These two poured their wisdom and love into those missionaries, and came home forever changed. This summer, five months later, they took the kids with them back to Italy to encourage and minister further to some of the same missionaries. And Matt and Robin played with missionary children and got close to them.

Now this fall these fun people have formed the "Encouragement International, Especially Italy, Organization," or, in short, "Ee Eye Ee Eye Oh"! The four of them hope to go once a year to Italy to have a continuing ministry to that particular mission field. And we're not talking tourist-vacationing; Myron and Gale have true "Barnabas" gifts of prayer concern and encouragement in the Lord.

Soon Matt and Robin will, too.

NOW WORK INTO YOUR LIFE
WHAT YOU'VE BEEN READING.

1. There's a crucially important concept in the first half of this chapter: "Become what you should be." How do you react to that? Does it sound discouraging, out of reach?

Read *Disciplines of the Heart* chapters 4 to 7: "Dare to believe your life could be wonderful" and "Learn to let God work in you." When your theology is right, you'll be full of optimism, hope, and expectations for yourself.

If you're in a study group, let that reading be a homework assignment; but for now read together, discuss, and take seriously—deeply believe—the following:

Philippians 1:10, 11; 2:15
Romans 6:6, 17, 18, 22.

2. Memorize Isaiah 33:6.

3. Think about a time in your life when you sinned and God inflicted pain! You discovered the hard way that the two go together. In a study group share your experiences.

Discuss types of punishment you've found effective to curb sin in your children at different age levels. Take notes, to listen and learn.

4. How can you become truly enthusiastic over your children, and how can you let them know it? (Resource: Anne Ortlund: *Children Are Wet Cement*, Fleming H. Revell, 1981.)

5. Pray for your family to experience regularly the "pleasure" of righteousness.

Slash the TV Watching

"I find television very educating. Every time some-body turns on the set I go into the other room and read a book."

—Groucho Marx

The psalmist David didn't like television any better than Groucho. Listen to what he wrote about it:

> I will walk in my house
> with blameless heart.
> I will set before my eyes
> no vile thing. (Ps. 101:2b, 3a)

Maybe he allowed Christian programs:

> My eyes will be on the faithful in the land,
> that they may dwell with me. (v. 6a)

But not just any Christian televangelists; David was choosy:

> He whose walk is blameless will minister to me. (v. 6b)

I think it was one of his first duties as soon as the kids were up to get the tube turned off:

> Every morning I will put to silence
> all the wicked of the land;
> I will cut off every evildoer. (v. 8)

I'm kidding, of course.

But, seriously, you can't be too careful. You can't shield the family's eyes from garbage too much. Not even the news, much of the time, is childproof. Think about how a little one hears these items:

"Fifty-one people were killed in a plane crash this afternoon."

"Some condoms have proved more effective than others."

"Last evening was fatal for a local woman and her son. Their mutilated bodies were found in the trunk of their car. There was evidence of sexual foul play."

Turn it off! "The world is too much with us." Even some cartoons can be hyper and trashy.

Says Dr. Armand Nicholi,

Most damage comes not from programs that directly attack the Christian faith or standards, but from those that make anti-Christian assumptions and whose attack is subtle and indirect.[1]

Dr. Saul Kapel says, "In recent seasons . . . we were offered hilariously funny episodes involving abortion, divorce, extramarital relationships, rape, and the ever-popular theme, 'Father is an idiot.'"[2]

And yet by the time the average American reaches age eighteen, he has spent 11,000 hours at school and 17,000 hours watching TV—the latter, the equivalent of nearly two years of his life![3]

---

1. Armand M. Nicholi III, "The Fractured Family," *Christianity Today,* 25 May 1979, [909] 11.
2. Quoted by Dr. James Dobson in *Focus on the Family* Magazine, Nov. 1988.
3. USA "Snapshots," *USA Today.*

Turn it off!

What kind of young person do you want to deploy into this needy world from *your* home? Somebody who's just like the world? If not, then get him off the diet of television, which is this world-system's chief mind-shaper and voice of propaganda, and feed him better things.

> "I want you to be wise about
> what is good, and innocent
> about what is evil" (Rom. 16:19).

Norman Corwin speaks of America as "a nation [that] has known greatness and stood as an exemplar to the world; . . . it has bred giants and accomplished prodigies." But trivializing influences have turned it away from all this, he writes, and gradually made it "indifferent, complacent, greedy, bored, hungry for kicks, amenable to getting-along-by-going-along, comfortable with mediocrity. . . ."

Trivializing causes damage in untold ways. It lowers sight; it crowds; it whittles away at our capacity to discriminate, to make choices, to have feelings.[4]

Through movies and television, children's senses get exposed to so much—the extremely dangerous, the totally shocking, the outrageously sleazy—that gradually they lose their ability to react. They get old too soon; they "know" too much: "toughly, smartly, sadly, wisely, agedly unenthralled"[5]—with jaded eyes still glued to the screen hoping the next joke will be funnier, the next behavior more bizarre. This is addiction: needing more and more input to produce the same kick.

And all their TV watching is damaging them physically as well. A just-released, ten-year study of 9.7 million kids

---

4. Norman Corwin, *Trivializing America* (Lyle Stewart Publ.) as cited in *Los Angeles Times*, 16 May 1984, V1.
5. Joyce Maynard, *Looking Back: A Chronicle of Growing Up Old in the Sixties,* as cited in the Corwin article, *Los Angeles Times*, 16 May 1984, V16.

from age six to seventeen says that their sedentary lifestyle is making them "fatter, not fitter":

- The number of physically "satisfactory" according to the test (which included sprints, sit-ups, push-ups, and long jumps) dropped from 43 percent ten years ago to 32 percent in 1989.
- Girls 12–17 take one minute longer to run a mile.
- The children average 14 pounds heavier, but they've lost cardiovascular endurance.

"The findings are ominous," says Dr. Wynn F. Updyke, director of the testing.[6]

Parent, understand what an enemy too much television is to much of what you're trying to accomplish in the home. It's an enemy of your children's bodies. It's an enemy of communication within the family. It's an enemy of play. It's an enemy of creativity. It's an enemy of time just to dream, to dillydally, to think one's own thoughts—so important for any child, to give his soul time to catch up to his body.

James Dobson shares a good idea in his book *Dr. Dobson Answers Your Questions:*

> I read about a system recently. . . . First it was suggested that parents sit down with the children and select a list of approved programs that are appropriate for each age level. Then type that list (or at least write it clearly) and enclose it in clear plastic so it can be referred to throughout the week.
> Second, either buy or make a roll of tickets. Issue each child ten tickets per week, and let him use them to "buy" the privilege of watching the programs on the approved lists. When his tickets are gone, then his television viewing is over for that week. . . . Ten hours a week is perhaps a good target to shoot at. . . .
> This system can be modified to fit individual home situations or circumstances. If there's a special program that all

---

6. *USA Today,* 15 Sept. 1989, 1A.

the children want to see, such as a Charlie Brown feature or a holiday program during Christmas and Thanksgiving, you can issue more tickets. You might also give extra tickets as rewards for achievement or some other laudable behavior.

Immediately, of course, you've got a problem. It's going to take plenty of emotional energy to fill in the gap left by vacated television. The pained cry day after day will be, "But, Mamma, what can I *do?*"

Well, there's dolls, tree climbing, jacks, books, hide-and-go-seek, "I spy," jumprope, dress-up, coloring and painting, building blocks, clay modeling, hopscotch, making up stories, putting on plays, biking, doll houses, stringing popcorn or paper strips, playing house, making doll clothes, touch football, sandlot baseball, playing with the garden hose in bathing suits, playing in the snow, baking cookies, recording on a cassette tape player, tricycles, wagons, trucks, paper dolls, making up an "amateur hour," selling lemonade, roller skating, walking the dog, organizing a secret club, mud pies, naps, or just sitting there staring. Just for starts.

PORTRAIT:
MORE ABOUT THE NORRISES

I was telling you about Dick and Mary Norris.

The Norrises picked with care the location in California where they wanted to raise their kids; the zoning laws had to be right.

The street where they lived looked like a typical suburban street, with big trees and one-story ranch homes. And theirs was a typical house on the block. It had a fairly small formal living room, a kitchen that opened onto a larger family room facing a pool outside, and side wings to the house that stretched a ways—including bedrooms for the parents and six kids plus working space for the family cookware business.

The pool area was typical, too. It looked like thousands of other California pools: no grass, just patio cement around it, and enclosed by a high fence.

Only one thing, if you were really alert, looked atypical: the fence had a little gate in the middle of the back of it. . . . What was this? You lifted the latch, pushed it open, and—

Rabbit hutches. Fat, sleek rabbits hunkered down inside.

Bantam chicken coops. Squawks, clucks, feathers—and a mild, not unpleasant, chicken smell.

Stretches of pasture.

Quackless ducks waddling around. Pheasants picking their way.

Two ponies tethered to posts!

One sheep!

Then you learned that Dick supervised the outdoor chores and Mary, the indoor. And you can bet, with all those pots and pans besides, there wasn't much time for television.

*   *   *   *   *

"The new American hearth, a center for family activities, conversation and companionship," announces *TIME* Magazine with irony and maybe sarcasm, "is the TV."[7]

Drastically change that! Drastically slash the television watching!

As Mark Twain said, "Whenever you find yourself on the side of the majority, it is time to pause and reflect."

---

7. *Time*, 27 Dec. 1982, 70.

NOW WORK INTO YOUR LIFE
WHAT YOU'VE BEEN READING.

The latest polling has just ascertained that the average American now watches television 7.02 hours daily, and as long as television has been in existence the hours graph has steadily climbed. To reverse this will indeed be drastic, and if there are two parents in your home, any new rules will call for shared decisions.

1. Thousands of wives feel lonely and cut off from communication because of their husbands' TV watching. Are you one of those?

How can you—

a. Be sensitive to his truly favorite programs and maybe share these with him?
b. Stay cheerful and positive—in the remote possibility that you're not as fun as television?
c. Plan activities together that you know he enjoys, to lure him away from his habit?
d. Determine to be gentle, realizing you at least know where he is, and things could be worse?

2. A generation of children has grown up not knowing the skills for play that children developed in pre-TV days. How can you help them learn? Would parties and group projects help?

3. Brainstorm with your friends, brainstorm in your study group, and pray!

Recoup Male and Female

"And here's the happy, bounding flea.
You cannot tell the he from she.
But she can tell, and so can he!"
—Roland Young

Maybe you've seen pictures of the sculpted crucifix in a major cathedral where the Christ sagging on the cross has male genitalia and female breasts. How sick, how pathetic.

Too many humans are wandering around these days having lost a strong sense of what all God's animals understand very well: the difference between male and female. Even lowly little fleas can make the distinction.

What happens when we humans start to blur the lines? Society goes bonkers. It's crucial today, in your very home, for father to "act father," mother to "act mother," and the boys to know they're future men, and the girls to know they're future women.

Of course God created the sexes equal, as Galatians 3:28 explains. And they're to receive equal consideration, equal respect, equal pay for equal work, and all the rest.

But they're different. And the differences must be clearly understood and followed.

69

```
┌─────────────────────────────┐
│         PORTRAIT:           │
│       THE BRAINARDS         │
└─────────────────────────────┘
```

Our friends Chuck and Sher have been married for a lot of years, and their two boys and one girl are now grown and out of the nest. Here's what Chuck and Sher are like.

Chuck likes to arrange flowers. Whenever they have company, Chuck does the table centerpiece. He also does all the home decorating at Christmas time, at Thanksgiving, and any other time he can think up an excuse. He picks out the wallpapers. He arranges and rearranges the furniture.

And then there's Sher. A while back Sher had a problem with the refrigerator, so she took it apart and put it back together again. All by herself she blacktopped their driveway. And when rains threatened a hillside in back of their home, guess who built a retaining wall? You got it: Sher.

But hey—like those happy, bounding fleas, Chuck and Sher both know very well that he's a he and she's a she. Chuck is a take-charge person—whether it's running the Presbyterian church where he's senior pastor, or arranging to lead Holy Land tours, or deciding which night light best fits the decor of the guest bathroom. And he took an active, firm hand in helping bring up the kids.

Sher is soft-spoken and pretty, hard-working and serene. She's no drudge, and she's no bore! She has a mind of her own and a lot of emotional strength to keep going their lovely home and social life and her first-lady duties at the church.

Chuck's a he; Sher's a she; they fit together fine. Just don't compare their biceps.

```
┌─────────────────────────────────────┐
│      WHAT GOD SAYS MEN ARE          │
└─────────────────────────────────────┘
```

The Bible reveals the rich heritage we have in the traditional behavior of good men. How much we owe them! The "faith of our fathers" is the strong underpinning of the whole Judeo-Christian social structure. Men whom we never saw were obedient to God's plans for them, and thereby established a godly precedent for succeeding generations of men, and their lingering influence is still our good foundation.

The Psalmist says, "In [God] our fathers put their trust" (Ps. 22:4). How did they express that trust?

Let's go back to Israel. Within that nation were tribes. Within the tribes were clans. Within the clans were families. And within each family was one man, the husband-father who stood in front of his family when the Israelites were called together—representing his family's rights and needs (Josh. 21:1, 2) and answering for their sins (Josh. 7:14, 15).

You see, God's idea of a good man isn't one who wears sweats and talks sports. Our friend Chuck would never qualify! God asks men—generally speaking, because there are exceptions—to assume leadership, and leadership is basically assuming responsibilities and jobs.

1. Salvation at Passover came as the dad of each household took his stand of obedience and faith for those under his roof (Exod. 12:3, 4). We can be grateful thousands did.

2. When God wanted a census taken, He ordered leading men from each tribe to supervise the headcount. The fellows obeyed and worked hard until the job was done (Num. 1:1–19).

3. It was the men who, by their organization, leadership, and labor, literally established the communities in the new Promised Land, as Moses said to them, "Build cities for your women and children, and pens for your flocks" (Num. 32:17).

4. It was the men whom God designated to do the dirty job of fighting for and protecting their families from all enemies (Num. 32:17).

5. And here's a tender word: When David had been away out of town he came home to "bless his household" (2 Sam. 6:20). (For many years, as Ray drove home from his duties through the streets of Pasadena, when he came to a certain lamppost, in his imagination he would hang all his problems on that post, and then drive into the garage and

walk into the house praying that he would be a blessing that evening to his household.)

Men are chosen by God to be men. Their manhood is a gift from Him, with all the rights, privileges, and responsibilities attached thereto. And God expects His men, under Himself, to love, protect, defend, and provide for the rest of His children.

God our heavenly Father created maleness, and He affirms it—just as any human father must affirm the maleness of his boys, teaching them manners, respect for women and girls, and care and defense of them at all costs. (His treatment of their mother will model all that.)

(I remember how thrilled I was in the third grade when two boys teased me, and my seventh-grade brother came along and discovered it, chased them, sat on them, and punched them good.)

Yes, in the beginning God our Father created maleness and also femaleness, and He pronounced them "very good." "Male and female he created them" (Gen. 1:27).

Two sexes provided for:

Procreation;

Interest, romance, and thrill;

Separate contributions to society's functioning;

And ever-new challenges to complement and encourage one another.

Three cheers, then, for all the good men who, under God, have sought to assume their responsibilities of leadership!
It ain't easy. "He that thinketh he leadeth, and hath no one following him—he is only out for a walk."

All leaders get their leadership tested—not only initially but periodically throughout their leadership.
I remember when Ray was burdened with the heavy duties of pastoring, and feeling a great need for the attention

and encouragement of his family, and he drove home one night and walked into the house and nobody really noticed. Nels was doing homework, I was busy studying. . . .

Ray said, "Hi, Nels." Nels said, "Hmmph."

Ray said, "Hi, Anne." I said, "Hmmph." (This is his version of the story.)

And Ray thought to himself, "This household doesn't need me. They're humming along just fine. If I didn't walk through the door some night, they'd never know the difference."

Ray took the reins of leadership; he called me to a Summit Meeting. And when he told me how lonely he felt and how unnecessary, I cried. I mean, I cried buckets! His impressions were 180 degrees from the truth, but I'd been insensitive and I hadn't realized his need.

And when I cried, Ray was thrilled! He had only been seeing me in my strengths—Mrs. C.E.O. of the Home, efficiently running a tight ship and keeping everything under control. But he hadn't seen me for too long a time in my weakness, my dependency on him (which was genuine), my need of him, my joy in him.

At our Summit Meeting we made some changes. I canceled some conferences and cut out some other obligations; I took new steps in giving my husband more time, more attention, more support. And it was interesting: when we both unburdened ourselves in our weaknesses, we experienced a closeness we'd never known before, and we fell in love all over again.

Our physical love began to take on new liberty and new excitement; we started to find new dimensions of delight in each other, and I believe I'm now more and more conscious of his needs—as he has always been of mine.

How important it was that night when Ray saw something wrong, for him not to back off or surrender to it but to roll up his sleeves and seek to make it right! Fifteen years later we're still reaping the benefits of that Summit Meeting.

Three cheers, too, for all the good men over the centuries who have loved their wives!

Larry Christensen writes,

> The love I have for my wife does not originate with me.
> It originates with God, and comes to me in the form of a
> command: 'Husband, love your wife."[1]

We know a fellow who, when he was young and idealis-
tic, married a girl with emotional problems. He knew he
loved her, and he figured his love would nurture her back
to health. On the contrary, her problems turned out to be so
serious, she's spent most of her adult life in a famous psy-
chiatric hospital. Rick has faithfully visited her over the
years, gently taken her out for drives or overnights or occasionally longer little stints, prayed for her, been true to her,
and fixed his eyes on the Lord in the hope of her eventual
release to live with him. His house stands ready. Rick's hair
is going from brown to grey. He still waits and loves.

Says Dietrich Bonnhoeffer, "It is not your love that sus-
tains marriage, but from now on it is your marriage that
will sustain your love." When lifelong commitment has
been sealed before God, then, as G. K. Chesterton says,
"that Thing marches on—that great, four-footed Thing, that
quadruped of the home!"

*And three cheers for all the good men who have commanded
their children!*

Now, if your family doesn't have that kind of father, all is
not lost. Timothy had a dad who was apparently "out of it"
spiritually (Acts 16:1). But his godly mother and grandmother made up the difference (2 Tim. 1:5), and Timothy
came to pastor with distinction the great Christian church
at Ephesus.

But God's normal way is for a man to command his children. Said the Lord about Abraham,

> I have chosen him, so that he will direct his children and
> his household after him, to keep the way of the Lord by
> doing what is right and just, so that the Lord will bring
> about for Abraham what he has promised him. (Gen. 18:19)

---

1. "The Christian Couple," *Bethany Fellowship Magazine,* 1977, 91.

A good father is

> Temperate, self-controlled, respectable, hospitable, able
> to teach, not given to much wine, not violent but gentle, not
> quarrelsome, not a lover of money. He must manage his
> own family well and see that his children obey him with
> proper respect. (1 Tim. 3:2–4)

"Able to teach . . . gentle. . . ." He's gracious, he's ac-
cessible, he's available.
Bill Cosby says,

> The father . . . must never say, "Get these kids out of
> here, I'm trying to watch TV." If he ever does start saying
> this, he is liable to see one of his kids on the six o'clock
> news.[2]

(Now, there's a threat for you.)

> Almost any man can be a father,
> but it takes someone special to be a daddy.

A good man is available. And he stoops. He's translatable
to his children's terms, on their level.
What a father God is! He has stooped through Jesus
Christ to our level and become translatable on our terms.
"As a father has compassion on his children, so the Lord has
compassion" (Ps. 103:13). The awesome Tetragrammaton,
that "Name" in Old Testament days which could not even
be pronounced, has now become for us "Abba"—Papa,
Daddy—so pronounceable that any little one can say it even
before he has teeth! How tender! And how tenderizing!

I watched a daddy in a restaurant the other day who had
taken his little bouncy-haired moppet out to lunch. He
leaned across the table and listened very seriously as she
showed him her doll and explained something I couldn't

2. *Fatherhood* (New York: Doubleday, 1986), 158.

hear but which took a very long time. He was meeting her on her terms.

That is, all but once when she had to meet him on his. In the middle of lunch she made another comment, and he gravely picked her up and carried her off to the men's room. . . .

To recap, *all honor and thanks to the good men who've been willing to shoulder leadership responsibility, who have loved their wives, and who have commanded their children.*

> Blessed is the man
> To whom his work is a pleasure,
> By whom his friends are encouraged,
> With whom all are comfortable,
> In whom a clear conscience abides,
> And through whom his children see God.[3]

WHAT GOD SAYS WOMEN ARE

And *three cheers for mother!* Over the centuries she's worked as hard as father, and for very different reasons.

He has built the houses; she's added the colors, the smells, the music.

He has shaped constitutions to make citizens protected; she has sewn flags to make them weep and cheer.

He has mustered armies and police forces to put down oppression; she has prayed for them and patted them on the back and sent them off with their heads up.

He has shaped decisions; she has added morale.

The first man kept a garden, and the first woman was made to be a help "meet"—suitable—for him (Gen. 2:18, KJV). (Does the word "help" sound demeaning? Our God Himself is often called the same word—our help—as in Psalm 33:20.)

---

3. Source unknown.

The woman in Proverbs 31 got up while it was still dark. She kept everybody fed and clothed. She bought fields. She planted vineyards. She brought in income. She cared for the poor. She was wise. She was busy. She was fun. She was a *help*, and everybody loved her for it.

What did her husband do? He sat at the city gates. Don't laugh. That was the heavy-duty place, the hot spot, the place of governmental and legal and administrative affairs.

Celebrate the mother! She, too, no less than the father, has, under God, shaped a magnificent human tradition.

God's first command to people was to "be fruitful and increase in number" (Gen. 1:28). She's been participating in the reproduction process ever since, through the pain of it and the pleasure. She's been obedient.

She was told to be a help suitable for the man, and for millennia she's been obedient to that, too—meeting spiritual needs and physical needs either by her own hands or by overseeing servants.

Even when Jesus walked this earth, it was women who ministered to His practical needs (Mark 15:40; Luke 8:1–3).

And in the early church, who was the woman most loved and honored? Dorcas, who "was always doing good and helping the poor" (Acts 9:36). And for two thousand years women have been living out 1 Timothy 5:10:

Bringing up children,

Showing hospitality,

Washing the feet of the saints (that is, caring for believers' practical needs),

Helping those in trouble,

And devoting themselves to all kinds of good deeds.

Good work, mothers! What would society have done without you need-meeters? Men have produced the machinery; women have put in the oil to keep it smooth-running. Hooray for you!

Napoleon was once asked what France most needed. His answer: "Mothers."

Said Abraham Lincoln, "All that I am or ever hope to be, I owe to my angel mother."

Amnon, Absalom, and Solomon all had the same father, David. Amnon and Absalom had heathen mothers; they turned out wicked. Solomon had a good mother; he turned out wise and wonderful.

Writes Gary Allen Sledge,

> It's difficult to know what counts in this world. Most of us count credits, honors, dollars. But at the bulging center of midlife, I am beginning to see that the things that really matter take place not in the board rooms, but in the kitchens of the world.[4]

Three cheers for women! Their contributions have been priceless.

But suddenly—really since World War II—our role as women is drastically changing. I see our greatest danger not in the new things we're stepping out and doing, but in the areas which as a consequence we're neglecting.

Titus 2:3–5 commands the younger women:

To love their husbands and children,

To be self-controlled and pure,

To be busy at home,

To be kind, and

To be subject to their husbands.

In these darkening "last days,"
Too many husbands and children are not loved.

---

4. Excerpted with permission from "The Woman in the Kitchen" by Gary Sledge *Reader's Digest,* September 1989. Copyright © 1989 by the Reader's Digest Assn., Inc.

Too many women are no longer "self-controlled and pure, . . . busy at home, . . . kind, . . . subject to their husbands."

And, remembering 1 Timothy 5:10,

Children are often not being truly "brought up."

Hospitality has dwindled.

Practical needs are not always being met.

Those in trouble are often neglected.

"All kinds of good deeds" frequently don't get done.

And citizens put more and more pressure on the government to meet these needs—because so many women have shifted to paying jobs and are no longer taking care of them.

Such a drastic change demands a drastic rethinking.

We must remember our original calling to be women.

Whatever the sacrifice, we must get back to the basics, to what God has called us to be and do as women—which only we, and nobody else, can be and do.

It's crucial today, in your very own home, for father to "act father," mother to "act mother," and the boys to know they're future men, and the girls to know they're future women.

NOW WORK INTO YOUR LIFE
WHAT YOU'VE BEEN READING.

Either on your own or in a group—
1. Notice descriptions of what God wants women to be and not be, do and not do. Make lists under those four categories:

Proverbs 11:16; 12:4; 14:1; 19:14; 21:9, 19; 31:10–31

Matthew 15:28

1 Corinthians 7:39

1 Corinthians 7:1–5

1 Corinthians 11:3; Eph. 5:22

1 Peter 3:1–4

Titus 2:3–5

2. How do you react to Ray's Summit Meeting, pages 72, 73? If you're a woman and married, do you tend, as I did, to be a functioning, insensitive, efficient "Mrs. C.E.O. of the Home"? How could that change?
3. Make a list of adjectives describing "what God says women are," pages 76–79. Rate yourself, on a scale of 1 to 10, against each of those adjectives. Have you a close friend who could pray for you concerning needy areas?
4. Society is desperately hurting these days from the blurring of male-female lines. Why don't you get on your knees about this, and intercede for society, and pray about what you can do to make a difference?

Take a Break

An imaginary session—some questions
to Anne and possible answers

Question One: Should we have children or not?
Answer: Well, to repeat what Clarence Day once said, "If
your parents didn't have any children, there's a good chance
that you won't have any."

But seriously, I hope I can convince you of the privilege
and wonder of producing and raising kids!

> Sons are a heritage from the Lord,
>   children are a reward from him. (Ps. 127:3)

> Our sons in their youth
>   will be like well-nurtured plants
> and our daughters will be like pillars
>   carved to adorn a palace. . . .
> Blessed are the people of whom this is true.
> (Ps. 144:12, 15)

Bruce Shelley has said this:

> A person has something in him that wants to continue
> after he's gone. And if it doesn't, he feels cheated, short-
> changed, outraged, defiled, corrupted, fragmented, injured.

Strong words! Maybe you don't feel like that now at all, if
you're young and both pulling in good salaries or getting
degrees and loving all the independence and the freedom.

But deeply, from the perspective of a long, full, human life—when God created people He made them "in His image." And as *He* is fulfilled in producing offspring (Eph. 1:23), so He made us to be the same.

Having children initiates you into an awesome circle. You join those who've become partners with God in creation.

> Your child has three parents: a mother, a father, and a heavenly Father (by creation if not by redemption). The three of you, together, created the precious package that was delivered into your arms on the day of your child's birth.[1]

You're saying, "But I see so much agony around me in raising kids."

"Making a decision to have a child," says Elizabeth Stone, "is momentous. It is to decide forever to have your heart go walking around outside your body."

But remember *these children are His,* and He cares even more than earthly parents care, and He shares the burden they are bearing. Again, when you parent, you join God in His very own occupation—parenting! And in a special way you enter into the recesses of the heart of God, when you suffer for sins not your own and rejoice in achievements and victories in which you only cooperated.

Is there any more important purpose for living in this world?

Q. But what right do we have to use up any more of nature's resources and pollute this world even more?

A. What if your own parents had asked that—?

Let's respect and enjoy this wonderful planet to the fullest, living as cleanly and thriftily and responsibly as we can while we do. ("Every litter bit hurts.") Train your children to do the same.

But may we never be horrified to discover that another precious human life has been conceived. China's one-child-per-family mandate is a tragic non-solution. God is populating heaven! Earth is only His vestibule, where He's getting His future citizens ready.

---

1. R. A. Scott, *Relief for Hurting Parents* (Nashville, TN: Oliver-Nelson), 62.

Q. But we just can't *afford* kids. We can barely pay the bills without them.

A. Back to Genesis 1. The command: "Be fruitful and increase in number" (v. 28).

The assurance in the very next verse:

> I give you every seed-bearing plant on the face of the whole earth and every tree that has fruit with seed in it. They will be yours for food. (v. 29)

Incidentally, later when the flood was over, God expanded that with "you've been vegetarians long enough":

> Everything that lives and moves will be food for you. Just as I gave you the green plants, I now give you everything. (Gen. 9:3)

Does that sound generous enough? Are you saying, "Still, that's just a worldwide principle. I'm talking about Cheryl and me. . . ."

Can you imagine an embarrassed God up there wringing His hands and saying, "I didn't mean *you*, Gus and Cheryl! I just meant all those other people!" If you wonder, check out Psalm 37:25, 26 and Psalm 145:15, 16 and many more of His promises to take care of His children.

Here's a principle you can count on:

Whatever God asks you to do, he'll supply every resource with which to do it.

And on that you can bet your last dollar.

(We're talking about reproduction, and I can't resist throwing in this little gem:

> They say a single oyster
> Lays a million eggs or two.
> Can you possibly imagine
> What a married one might do?

—Agnes W. Thomas)

Question Two: What shall I do with my impossible teenagers?

Answer: Here's what a typical teenager is like:

A teenager is . . .

A person who can't remember to walk the dog but never forgets a phone number.

A weight watcher who goes on a diet by giving up candy bars before breakfast.

Someone who can hear a song by Madonna played three blocks away but not his mother calling from the next room.

A whiz who can operate the latest computer without a lesson but can't make a bed.

A student who will spend twelve minutes studying for her history exam and twelve hours for her driver's license.

A connoisseur of two kinds of fine music, loud and very loud.[2]

But there are reasons why our teenagers are the way they are.

Teenagers are people in transition. You and I have made enough transitions, even in our adult lives, to know how unstable they are, and how confused and depressed losses and gains can make us. Expect these kids to be restless, temperamental, critical of their present situation, and experimental—wanting to push outward and flex their muscles, and yet inside, scared to death to do it.

It's normal for them to go through stages of not liking you. Well, sometimes *you* go through stages of "not liking you," too! Tell them so. Marriages go through the same ebb and flow. You all just hang in there together because you're the *Joneses* or whoever—and no matter what others may do, the Joneses stick together.

When the feelings of closeness are there between spouse and spouse, between parents and children, between children and children—great! Enjoy them. If the "feelings" go for a while, you're still on the same territory and nobody's going to bolt. Say so—over and over. You're building in stability every time you do. And affirm the fact that the good feelings will later return; then you're also building in hope.

___
2. *What Is a Teenager?* (Bill Adler Books, 1986).

They don't have to like you, they only have to function as kids in the home and cooperate. You don't have to like *them* sometimes, either—but you have to go right on functioning as a parent and cooperating. That's the Joneses' style. You've all got staying power for the long haul, because it's gonna get *good*. Really good. Tell them so! Spell it out frequently, with words and hugs.

Be sympathetic to their scholastic struggles.

Aaron Schmidt, as a high school senior, did some pretty heavy research and wrote an essay with real insights about his age:

> There are four levels of thinking, and, to make it brief, kids my age are treated as if we are on the highest level of thinking, which is the "formal" level. On this level you should be able to figure out all kinds of things. The problem is that most kids my age and even a lot of adults are only in the third stage, which is the "concrete" stage! Guess what level most of the school materials are on? Right! The "formal" level! No wonder we can get so bogged down.
>
> A man named Dr. Epstein has also figured out some facts about us. He has discovered that our brain grows at different times! That is really awesome! During the years from two to four, six to eight, ten to twelve, and fifteen to seventeen, our brain is growing and it makes it easier to learn.
>
> Notice that around thirteen and fourteen it isn't growing? Well, this is the time that most work is given to us in junior high and usually on that "formal" level! That's two strikes against us. I don't even have to tell you what grades in school most kids fail.[3]

It makes you begin to understand a conversation like the one I once read in the *New Yorker*:

Teenager: "Is Paris in England?"
Friend: "No, Paris is in France."
Teenager: "Oh, well, I never was very good at geometry."

---

3. Aaron Schmidt, "The 'Range of the Strange,'" *Stillpoint* Magazine, summer 1988, 19, 20.

You laugh. Would you want to go back to school with them and try to pass all their tests?

> Half of all high school students have trouble with basic math. That means that out of fourteen million students . . . uh . . . uh. . . . [4]

Question Three: If our kids rebel, will they eventually return to our values?

Answer: Dr. James Dobson surveyed 853 parents and found, at the time of the polling, 85 percent success. Fifty-three percent of the young people had come back "home" to the values of their folks, and 32 percent more now somewhat accept their values. Of the 15 percent holdouts? Well, there's still time. The last chapter of their lives hasn't been written yet. Let that encourage you.

Our own four children, all out of the nest and all four in ministry, are close and enthusiastically going the same direction as their parents. Just the same, each has his own quirk of theological differences. Ray's comment: "We taught our kids to think for themselves, and doggone if they didn't go and do it!"

Question Four: Let's talk about the whole process of our kids' finding marriage partners.

Answer: Don't be too eager to get rid of them. Put from your mind the little thought, "Oh, boy, a guest room." Whom they marry means everything, in shaping the continuum of your family life and family contribution to the world. You want to pass your families' values on to the next generation.

> From everlasting to everlasting.
>   the Lord's love is with those who fear him,
>   and his righteousness with their children's children.
>   (Ps. 103:17)

> We your people, the sheep of your pasture,
>   will praise you forever;
> from generation to generation
>   we will recount your praise. (Ps. 79:13)

---

4. Sue Sebesta in *Quote Magazine.*

(Wouldn't it be exciting to work this last verse, Psalm 79:13, into a family crest with your family name, to be placed over your fireplace mantel for the kids to grow up under? If you have more than one child, some day you might have to have duplicates made, to put over each of their mantels! "Let this be written for a future generation, that a people not yet created may praise the Lord" [Ps. 102:18].)

Ray and I believe that God has a specific mate He's preparing—if they marry at all—for each of your children. Otherwise, why would He spend all of Genesis 24 detailing the specifics of procuring a very particular wife for Isaac? In each marriage He's choosing to put certain genes together, certain ministries together. He knows His ongoing plans.

In your young people's dating years, encourage Christian friends and Christian dates. Depending on the stability of your kids right then, maybe you can't insist. But hopefully as they approach serious-dating years you're getting closer again, and you can talk things over. Let them know it makes a big long-range difference whether the parents really approve or not of their in-law children.

> Esau . . . married Judith, daughter of Beeri the Hittite, and also Basemath, daughter of Elon the Hittite. They were a source of grief to Isaac and Rebekah. (Gen. 26:34, 35)

Painful years passed. . . .

> Then Rebekah said to Isaac, "I'm disgusted with living because of these Hittite women." (Gen. 27:46)
> Esau then realized how displeasing the Canaanite women were to his father Isaac. . . . (Gen. 28:8)

A family is a *family.* It's a unit. It has personality. It has structure. Additions have to fit. But finding those new additions is often a tricky thing. Thumbs-up or thumbs-down decisions on your part shouldn't come too fast. Ray and I have been known to get convinced and change our minds, and the kids' choices turned out to be exactly right.

I also remember my own parents weren't exactly thrilled over Ray. Poor boy! I think no man would ever really have been good enough for their precious firstborn daughter. And although I had graduated from college, and Ray was older yet and in the Navy and able to support me, still we postponed our marriage for a whole, very long, year until my parents knew we really meant it.

They, too, got thoroughly persuaded in succeeding years. They couldn't have been prouder as their son-in-law, at age thirty-five, was called to pastor a large church. But we've been glad, in the long run, that we moved slowly and received their blessing.

Q. What are the criteria for mates for our kids?

A. There seem to be only two thoroughly spelled out in the Bible.

One, believers are to marry believers (2 Cor. 6:14, 15).

Two—and this one's more complicated—they shouldn't marry divorced people (Rom. 7:2, 3). There could be two exceptions here, and sincere Bible students have differing opinions about them.

First Corinthians 7:12–15 seems to allow room for divorce from an unbeliever who walked out because of the spouse's faith. Matthew 5:32 seems to permit it if there was "marital unfaithfulness." You'd have to ask, "Has this person's church investigated and approved the reason for the divorce, and do they give full permission for the remarriage?" The opinions of the pastor and godly elders of the church should make a difference.

Beyond that, marrying within your race, whatever your race may be, can make adjustments easier (Gen. 24:1–4). Just practically, the closer the two are culturally, the easier the fitting together. . . .

But give them space. It's no time to "hover." That can discourage them from ever finding anybody at all.

Question Five: You apparently approve of birth control. Then how did your own children get spaced the way they did? I've heard you say that Sherry was born ten months after you were married, and Margie eleven months after that, and Ray, Jr., seventeen months later, and then fifteen years later you had Nels. Is that a little weird?

Answer: Sorry, we've just run out of time. Thank you very much.

Take a Break II

Marriage-family jokes I couldn't find a place for in this book

Izzy's wife died. They'd been married for many years. It was a big funeral.

The next day the rabbi thought he'd pay Izzy a call at his home to console him. When he pushed open the door, there was Izzy on his couch kissing a gorgeous redhead!

"Izzy!" cried the rabbi. "What are you thinking, with your beloved wife of so many years barely cold in her grave?"

Izzy cried, "In grief should I know what I'm doing?"

*   *   *   *   *

"Sweetheart," cried the enthusiastic honeymooner, "I couldn't live without you. If you ever leave me, I'm coming along!"

*   *   *   *   *

A fellow told his doctor he just couldn't do all the things around the house that he used to do. When the examination was finished he said,

"Now, Doc, I can take it. In plain English, what's wrong with me?"

"There's nothing wrong," said the doctor. "In plain English, you're lazy."

"Okay, Doc," said the fellow. "Now give it to me in medical terms so I can tell my wife."

* * * * *

"We have found the secret of a happy marriage. It's dinner out twice a week by candlelight and soft music. This is followed by a nice, slow walk home.
"She eats out on Tuesdays, and I eat out on Fridays."[1]

POST SCRIPT

If you're studying this book in a group, why don't you "take a break" with this chapter and have a party, or at least loosen up for a more fun time together?

Read "Take a Break" on the spot, if you like, or just assign it for homework.

Definitely read "Take a Break II" together, and add all the other family jokes you can think of. Hey, if they're really good, send them to me so I can laugh, too. My address is at the end of this book.

---

1. Bob Phillips in the Foreword to *If Mr. Clean Calls, Tell Him I'm Not In* by Martha Bolton (Ventura, CA: Regal, 1989), 8.

Teach Respect

"A man's children and his garden both reflect the amount of weeding done during growing season."

Everybody's concerned about the eroding influence of authority figures: the police, the military, the church Catholic or Protestant, the courts, the schools.

But basic to them all, behind them all, *whose clout is really being challenged? The man's clout.*

And I see the woman as the key to rectifying that.

What's the current Dad fad? Television gives some clues:

Roseanne: "You may marry the man of your dreams, ladies, but fifteen years later you're married to a reclining chair that burps."

Or to her TV son: "You're not stupid. You're just clumsy like your daddy."

Cereal commercial: Husband and wife are playing tennis. She never misses a shot. Mr. Dork, though, lets a ball hit him right on the head. Presumably because he didn't eat the right cereal.

Airline commercial: Two reporters from competing newspapers are chatting. He: "I read your story this morning. You scooped me again." She: "I didn't know you could read."

92

Razor commercial: A gal dressed in a formal literally smacks a guy in a tuxedo across the face. If he were a member of any minority group—woman, black, gay, retarded, senior citizen—can you imagine the outrage, the hullabaloo, the lawsuits? But a man is fair game.[1]

Says Dr. James Dobson,

Respect for leadership is the glue that holds social organization together. Without it there is chaos, violence, and insecurity for everyone.[2]

"Respect for leadership!" He's right.
And perhaps the initiator of it all, the one from whose respect all the rest of respect emanates, is the wife in the home. God gives in Ephesians 5:33 this crucial instruction:

The wife must respect her husband.

What is God saying to the wife? He's saying,
Back off. Down, girl!
Don't be forever challenging him, criticizing him, contradicting him, interrupting him, deriding him, competing with him, negating him, scolding him, doubting him, overriding him.
In the Amplified Bible Ephesians 5:33 reads like this:

And let the wife see that she respects and reverences her husband—that she notices him, regards him, honors him, prefers him, venerates and esteems him; and that she defers to him, praises him, and loves and admires him exceedingly.

Ephesians 5:33 ought to be a conscious, daily discipline. And it ought to be physical as well as verbal! A marriage can get delicious when the wife begins to enjoy every part of her husband's body—and then begins to remind him

---

1. Bernard R. Goldberg, "Television Insults Men, Too," the *New York Times*, 14 March 1989.
2. James Dobson, *Dare to Discipline* (Wheaton, IL: Tyndale House—Regal Books, 1970), 88.

over and over of all his parts and all his qualities in which she delights!

(For wonderful models, go back to the conversations between the lovers in Song of Solomon.)

She's choosing to ignore his weaknesses and admire his strengths. (Of course he has plenty of both.) She's training herself to put him up, not down. It's a key "discipline of the home."

Shirley Scott says, "I was visiting friends who'd just celebrated their 54th wedding anniversary. The husband tramped in from work leaving clods of dirt on the carpet. I said, 'His boots certainly bring the dirt in.' 'Yes,' she smiled, and went for the vacuum, 'but they bring him in, too.'"[3]

With this kind of mindset a wife is obeying Ephesians 5:33, and she's strengthening her own personal happiness, her marriage, her family life, her kids, and ultimately society.

You see, the wife who challenges, contradicts, doubts, overrides, and negates her husband will probably produce offspring who later challenge teachers, contradict government, doubt laws, override police, negate courts, and in general produce a hassled, ineffective, exhausted society. If father has no clout, eventually neither does anyone else.

On the other hand, when the wife, by an act of her will and in obedience to Ephesians 5:33, decides to continually and enthusiastically respect and support her husband, a whole chain reaction goes into place:

The children learn to respect Dad and Mom, too. They "honor father and mother."

Dad grows in stature; he changes; he may well *become what they're claiming him to be.*

He also begins to respect and praise Mom (Prov. 31:28).

And the children are on the road to respecting all government authorities, as Romans 13:1 commands.

The respectful woman is eventually an important key to the success of all society.

---

3. From an old quote I received years ago. Source unknown.

I love being a woman right now to say these things. When men teach the same thing, somebody's apt to call them power-hungry chauvinists. (And some of them are, but maybe they've become like that because of aggressive women in their lives who've challenged their every toehold of leadership.)

Says our heavenly Father in statements that are blatantly sexist,

> Adam was formed first, and then Eve. (1 Tim. 2:18)

> The head of the woman is man. (1 Cor. 11:3)

To praise, enjoy, be comfortable with, and yes, follow these guys in our lives has got to be a voluntary thing. "You first, honey. . . . You first, my brother." Easy or not, it must initiate with us women.

Will this attitude produce insipid doormats? Yes, it will and often does—in vast areas of the world where it's merely a cultural tradition. And then enormous reservoirs of brains and gifts are wasted and lost.

But if a woman's "you first" is a spiritual decision, then it's simply saying that God calls the shots. In that case, one of two things will happen.

One, she'll learn to follow with grace and poise. And, generally speaking, she'll be honored and elevated and her gifts fulfilled in every way, because her unthreatening, encouraging attitude will evoke a similar response in the male.

Or two, the Lord may sovereignly choose to set aside the rules and appoint her a judge like Deborah, or a prophetess like one of Philip's daughters, or a corporation president, or who knows what. She'll be ready for whatever God plans.

```
PORTRAIT:
CURT AND LORI
```

Lori is tall and angular and coordinated. She strides like the athlete she is, and she runs her fingers through her fashionably short haircut, and she laughs a lot. Lori was a straight-A student at a tough private college, and her round, blue eyes look right at you with no apology when she carries on a very sharp conversation. And in no time you see that she's strongly opinioned and precisely directional.

Lori is a leader if ever you saw one.

But Lori is also married to a leader—one who is also big and strongly opinioned and precisely directional. Curt could have had his pick of lots of girls in our church; he was a full-time pastor on staff and definitely our most eligible bachelor. Curt didn't pick a little petunia; he picked Lori.

She could have clashed with him at every turn; maybe she has. But anyone who knows Lori knows how affirming and encouraging she's become. Maybe this side of her was forged on the anvil of real agonies behind the scenes—I don't know. Any great marriage calls for all the tough disciplines we can muster.

I only know that Curt and Lori have a great marriage. She tells him over and over how wonderful he is, and she tells everybody else the same thing. And Curt is wonderful.

Curt's response? He tells Lori over and over how wonderful she is, and he tells everybody else how wonderful Lori is! And he's right; she's wonderful.

A little sickening, you say? Listen, it's worse than that: they have two tall, handsome teenagers who are proud of how wonderful their parents are.

A PORTRAIT FOR THE BIRDS

Sand hill cranes are very special. They can fly in their formations for longer distances and over longer periods of time than any other crane known.

Apparently there are three reasons why.

First, they rotate their leadership so that no single crane gets too tired. Second, they choose only their strongest cranes for leadership, to buffet those fierce wind currents.

And third, all the time the leader is leading, all the other cranes behind him are continually and noisily honking, honking, their enthusiasm and admiration and approval!

NOW WORK INTO YOUR LIFE
WHAT YOU'VE BEEN READING.

1. God considered Leviticus 19:3a so important for the Israelites that He built in the ultimate punishment for violators: Leviticus 20:9! Why do you think God thought this respect was so crucial?

Notice how He coupled this respect with respect for Himself: Leviticus 19:32. Incidentally, do you teach this respect to your children?

And notice whom else your children must respect:

1 Timothy 3:4

1 Thessalonians 5:12, 13

1 Peter 2:17

God also says whom the father must respect:

1 Peter 3:7

2. If you're a wife, on a scale of 1 to 10, how do you rate your obedience to Ephesians 5:33b? In your notebook write measurable ways you can improve, and begin today!

In a group discuss these new intentions—and be accountable to report next time how you're doing.

THE SEVENTH DRASTIC DO

Teach Values

"As the twig is bent, the tree inclines."
—Virgil, 70–19 B.C.

"Without God, we cannot. Without us, He will not."
—St. Augustine of Hippo, A.D. 354–430

What do we do with these fascinating, intimidating off-spring? We put values into them as faithfully as we put in vitamins and food and sleep. We're fighting off death, and values are life-giving.

Said Romain Roland, "France fell because there was corruption without indignation."
And King Solomon wrote,

My son, pay close attention to what I say;
   listen closely to my words.
Do not let them out of your sight,
   keep them within your heart. . . .

When you walk, they will guide you;
   when you sleep, they will watch over you;
   when you awake, they will speak to you.
For these commands are a lamp,
    this teaching is a light,
    and the corrections of discipline are the way to life.
      (Prov. 4:20; 6:22, 23)

Teaching values means saying, "This is bad, this is good. Hate the bad, cling to the good." (See Rom. 12:9.) By word and by example, you set the bad on the left, you set the good on the right, and you say, "See that bad? Don't touch it with a ten-foot pole. See that good? Go after it!"

At every state of their development, over and over and over.

Look how love is defined in 1 Corinthians 13, and you get an insight into values.

GOOD	BAD

Love . . .

Its opposite . . .

1. is patient, "waits on the Lord"	1. is impatient, self-willed, demands instant gratification
2. is kind, compassionate	2. is abusive, vengeful
3. does not envy, has a spirit of gratitude and contentment	3. wants what others have
4. does not boast, is modest, possesses true humility	4. brags, showcases himself
5. is not proud, takes his place, acknowledges authority	5. considers himself autonomous, demands all his rights
6. is not rude but courteous	6. is ungracious, indifferent to others' needs
7. is not self-seeking but is fulfilled in helping others	7. loves to improve himself, do good to himself, accumulate
8. is not easily angered but is self-controlled, temperate	8. has a hot temper, is easily frustrated
9. keeps no record of wrongs, has a forgiving spirit	9. has a long memory of others' faults, tends to seek to "pay back"

GOOD	BAD

Love . . .

Its opposite . . .

10. does not delight in evil but rejoices with the truth; is discerning, sees the difference, has deliberately chosen good

10. is naive, permissive, accepts both good and bad, has a weak sense of values

11. always protects, tries to shield the vulnerable

11. looks out only for himself

12. always trusts, considers someone "innocent until proven guilty," gives the benefit of the doubt

12. has a suspicious nature, concludes the worst, is gossipy, adversarial

13. always hopes, is optimistic

13. tends to worry, be faithless, pessimistic

14. always perseveres, is willing to suffer to see things through

14. tries to avoid pain at all cost, quits and starts easily

Live and teach good values, constantly and consistently—

so that you, your children and their children after them may fear the Lord your God as long as you live . . . so that you may enjoy long life, . . . so that it may go well with you and that you may increase greatly. . . .

Impress them on your children. Talk about them when you sit at home and when you walk along the road, when you lie down and when you get up. (Deut. 6:2, 3, 7)

"I have now disposed of all my property to my family," wrote Patrick Henry. "There is one thing more I wish I could give them, and that is the Christian religion."

Think about these virtues of 1 Corinthians 13.

---

1. "Love is patient."
Becka and Frank and their three children were squeezed into a second-floor condo, and they couldn't afford to move

until Frank got a promotion at work. Frank's company was full of rivalry and politics, and Frank refused to enter in to all that. He just held his head up and did his job, and the two of them waited on God. Most of the time they really didn't fret; they figured God's schedule was better than theirs.

Let me tell you something about Becka. She was a first-born baby who arrived when feeding on demand was the "in" thing; but Becka's parents philosophized that they didn't want to give Baby the impression that she was the center of the universe, and that humans would always drop everything to meet her needs. So when Becka cried off schedule her mother made sure that she was okay, and then let her cry. Becka learned early to "fit in"; she learned contentment; she enjoyed the rhythms of regular living.

Maybe this contributed to her patience regarding Frank's job—trusting that God's timing was better than her own.

> I have stilled and quieted my soul;
>   like a weaned child with its mother,
>   like a weaned child is my soul within me. (Ps. 131:2)

> My soul waits for the Lord
>   more than watchmen wait for the morning,
>   more than watchmen wait for the morning. (Ps. 130:6)

Eventually God gave Frank a remarkable promotion, at close to twice the salary. They've moved into a home, with room for entertaining and for the children to play.

> Blessed are all who wait for him! (Isa. 30:18)

"Love is patient."

---

4. *"Love does not boast."* It's modest; it possesses true humility.

A hawk came swooping low over the jungle boasting, "I'm invincible! Nobody can touch me!"

A lion was roused by this and roared, "No, *I'm* invincible! Nobody can touch me!"

A skunk heard the roar and raised its head and said, "I think *I'm* invincible! Nobody can touch me!"

But then along came a cobra and swallowed them all up—hawk, lion, and stinker. Oh-oh. Bad joke.

Boasting never pays.

We parents need to learn this. We're in a competitive world that uses every phony trick to capture others' imagination, even their jealousy. Love is what they really want most, but they're often totally ignorant of how to get it.

Puff yourself, and you get admiration—or maybe envy. Deflate yourself and you get love. You can enjoy ever-deepening friendships all your life if you'll expose yourself, be vulnerable, be willing to let your weaknesses show.

The same is true in handling each other as a married couple, and in handling the children.[1]

Last night Nels came down from Pasadena where he lives and works, to stay with us overnight. He and his friend and I went to see that fascinating movie *The Dead Poets' Society.* It reminded Nels of all his schooling years, and he said he felt we'd put him in the wrong elementary schools. I defended what we did. And so we went to bed.

I couldn't sleep.

This morning I had to say it to him: "Nels, my big mouth did it again! You were expressing some legitimate hurts last night, and it was time for me just to listen to your feelings. It wasn't the time for me to justify myself."

I went on to say, "I goofed a lot in raising you, and I'm still at it, and I apologize. You've turned out wonderfully well—not because of me but in spite of me!"

There were hugs, kind words, and all was well.

"All have sinned and fall short of the glory of God" (Rom. 3:23)—every member of the family. "All we like sheep have gone astray" (Isa. 53:6). We're all in this together.

We need to say so. Humility is more caught than taught.

"Love does not boast."

---

1. See Anne Ortlund's books *Children Are Wet Cement* (Old Tappan, NJ: Revell, 1978) and *Building a Great Marriage* (Old Tappan, NJ: Revell, 1985).

5. *"Love is not proud."* It takes its place; it acknowledges authority.

If a child gets no authority and no love, he may turn into a monster.

If he gets authority but no love, he may turn into a cringer.

If he gets love but no authority, he may turn into a tyrant.

But if he gets both love and authority, he may well become whole. When he learns to embrace both, over the long haul he'll learn to love his parents. He'll sing his alma mater with gusto. He'll salute the flag, maybe sometimes with tears in his eyes. He'll love God!

What if his country asks him to go to war? Well, he did difficult things his parents asked of him. He got used to *authority plus love,* and it put nerve and grit into him.

What if God asks him to die for his faith? Said Job, "Though he slay me, yet will I trust him" (Job 13:15).

Authority with love, when a child is small, sows the seeds of a great patriot, a great world-citizen, a great Christian.

Then point out policemen as his friends. Speak well of city officials ("don't they keep our streets clean?"). Pray together for state and national leaders (1 Tim. 2:1, 2).

When your youngster has a run-in with a teacher, a youth sponsor, the pastor—easy does it. Point out they have a tough job. Read together 1 Thessalonians 5:12, 13.

Don't ever have "roast preacher" for Sunday dinner. From his lips your child hears the Word of God. Don't spoil that!

And as your young person becomes a citizen of this world, teach him—

To obey government leaders: Romans 13:1, 2.

To pay whatever taxes they ask: Romans 13:7.

Not to speak against them: Titus 3:1, 2.

To obey even bad governments under normal conditions: 1 Peter 2:13–20 (remembering the Caesars under whom these words were written).

Show your older children what unbelievers will be like in the last days before Christ returns: 2 Timothy 3:1–5 (disobedient to parents) and 2 Peter 2:10–12 (despising authorities).

Gradually over his teen years, be weaning him from your authority to God's, from exterior to interior. When you're finally done with him, he'll be inner-directed; his first love and his first authority will both be God.

"Love is not proud." It takes its place. It acknowledges authority.

---

7. *"Love is not self-seeking."* It's fulfilled in helping others.

I sat in a Bible conference once listening to a missionary doctor from Africa. He told of driving a jeep all one night to take a woman back from the hospital to the village where she lived. There didn't seem to be anyone else to do it, and she had to go home, so he took her. The rain never let up once during that long, dark night, during that entire round trip, and part of the way the roads were almost impossible.

By the time he got back it was dawn. He was soaked, muddied, exhausted. He showered and went to work. Nobody at the hospital all day thanked him, nobody commended him, and this doctor simply had to pray, "Lord, that trip was for You. I'm glad the woman could get home, but I really did it for You, and Your commendation is enough."

When we go to our daily round of tasks in the home, together as a family, we go as servants. We don't protect ourselves. And for us parents God's commendation is enough. The children need their parents' praises—often and enthusiastically—until they're grown up and their heavenly Parent's approval will be enough.

Here's a Drastic Do for you: *teach your children to work.* When they're little, give them little jobs around the house. When they're bigger, give them bigger ones.

Maybe put a sign on their wall, "You can't have bread and loaf!"

Launch them into the world expecting to serve, not to be served—to please others, not just to please themselves.

"Love is not self-seeking."

---

10. "Love does not delight in evil but rejoices with the truth."
It discerns, it sees clearly the difference between evil and
truth, and then deliberately chooses truth.

Discernment is picking your way carefully along that cov-
eted goal of godliness. Having examined the alternatives, it
sees what will get you where you want to go.

Said Joshua to the children of Israel,

> Now fear the Lord and serve him with all faithful-
> ness. . . . But if serving the Lord seems undesirable to
> you, then choose for yourselves this day whom you will
> serve. . . .
> But as for me and my household, we will serve the Lord.
> (Josh. 24:14, 15)

Discernment isn't having a seeing-eye dog, it's having a
seeing eye. Make it your goal to bring your young people to
the point where they're no longer dependent on the guidance of others; they can see for themselves the right thing
to do.

This last attribute of love really sums up all the others. It
says, "Look at right values, look at wrong values, and choose
the right."

The choosing is the tough part, the part that takes
courage. Tell your kids how teenager Daniel, under great
pressure, "resolved not to defile himself" (Dan. 1:8).

Tell them what Paul wrote to young Timothy:

> Don't let anyone look down on you because you are
> young, but set an example for the believers in speech, in
> life, in love, in faith and in purity. (1 Tim. 4:12)

Paul was teaching values!

At every stage of your offspring's life—the baby, the
toddler, the pre-teen, the teenager, the young adult—you
do the same.

No adult or child ever got lost on a straight and narrow road.

NOW WORK INTO YOUR LIFE
WHAT YOU'VE BEEN READING.

1. Chapter 11 of Hebrews is a series of stories of people who by faith turned their backs on poor values and chose worthy ones.

From verses 4 to 12 you have five illustrations of making right choices over wrong. Who were they, and what did they turn from, and what did they choose?

Verses 13 to 16 summarizes what they were doing in making right value choices.

Verses 23 and following give more illustrations. What are they?

2. Now Hebrews 12:1, 2 tells you to turn from bad values and choose good ones. What are you to repudiate? What are you to embrace?

3. What can you do to teach your children to do the same?

4. We're discussing here a life-and-death matter. Spend a good time in prayer about your own choices of God's values, and your influence on your children and others.

THE EIGHTH DRASTIC DO

Believe God

I. FAITH FOR THE PARENTS

"We have nothing to fear but fear itself."
—Franklin D. Roosevelt

If you're a typical Christian today, with a typical Christian family, you're standing at a crossroads with a choice between fears and faith.

Do you want a family life that's distinguished by joy? Do you want an atmosphere of well-being and rest of heart and confidence and fun? Do you want a lot of laughter at your house? And doesn't it seem as if that's really the way a good Christian home ought to be?

If you sense yours isn't like that, you could have caught the disease that's rampant these days in Christian households—the disease of fear.

God never intends your house to be fearful. There are 365 "fear nots" in the Bible—one for every single day of the year.

Some insights in this chapter were gleaned from sermons I heard—one each by Dr. Stanley Mooneyham (re. wheat and tares) at Palm Desert Community Church, Palm Desert, CA, June 12, 1989, and Dr. John R. Claypool (re. Joseph) at Princeton Theological Seminary, June 27, 1988.

Let me suggest three fears that commonly plague believers these days.

1. *Christian parents may have an unhealthy fear of the school system.* Everywhere Ray and I go we see them—mostly mothers—absolutely exhausted from home schooling, parents who aren't educationally or emotionally equipped to take over this huge, important task. Or we see them tense from debt because they've put their kids into Christian schools when financially they had no business doing it.

This is not a plea for public schools. God will lead you to the best schooling for each of your children, and the answer may be different for each. Certainly home schooling is a good opportunity for far more togetherness, influence, and bonding, and Christian schools are a way of exposing your children to the reinforcement of Christian values.

This isn't a plea for public schools, it's a plea for you to examine your heart to see if you're making decisions based on your fears or based on your faith.

Studies have shown that the home is by far the greatest influence on children, and if they're active in a good church, the church influence comes in strongly second. (I personally had only the first; my family seldom lived where there was a good church. But I had strongly godly parents, and all four of us children turned out totally the Lord's.)

What children do *not* need put into their heads is a spirit of unhealthy suspicion and fright.

> For God did not give us a spirit of timidity, but a spirit of love and of self-discipline. (2 Tim. 1:7)

It will take their whole childhoods to complete the job of encouraging them (and you'll temporarily back off when they're temporarily fragile), but as a general rule teach your children to go into the world strongly, as a confident minority, with their heads up.

Let them walk into it as Daniel's three friends walked into the fiery furnace (and they were probably teenagers themselves, or not much more). When the king peered into the fire he saw not three people but four—halleluia for the fourth, "Immanuel"! There they were, walking around in the fire "unbound and unharmed" (Dan. 3:25).

Tell your children over and over that One walks with them through all this world's judgment fires, and that this "one who is in [them] is greater than the one who is in the world" (1 John 4:4). They are to be free and unscathed, "unbound and unharmed."

Christian parents, give thanks every morning with your children for the privilege of school (so many children in the world never get to learn to read and write and have knowledge opened up to them!). Pray for His protection over them, pray that they'll be good witnesses that day for Jesus, and send them off with hearts full of trust in the Lord.

> Security is not the absence of
> danger but the presence of God

2. *Christian parents may have an unhealthy fear of foods.* This is another fear currently nearing epidemic stage. Believers as well as others can be absolutely paranoid over what they might put into their mouths.

Wrote Jack Sharkey,

> Jack Sprat could eat no fat,
> His wife could eat no lean.
> A real sweet pair of neurotics!

Recently the Washington *Post* said it like this:

Americans are engulfed in an epidemic—not of cancer but of fear. However, many scientists say obsessive reliance on bottled water and organic products is foolish. Instead, Americans should devote more concern to three things that cause the vast majority of premature deaths: alcohol, tobacco and over-consumption of saturated fats.

"Driving a car is pretty risky compared with, say, drinking apple juice with a trace of Alar in it," says Prof. Richard Wilson of Harvard University and an expert in comparing risks. The average American is thousands of times more

likely to die in a car wreck than of cancer from pesticides.
But in interviews with 25 shoppers buying organic produce
at a local supermarket, nearly half said they had not worn
their seat belts on the way to the store.

"People have an inappropriate sense of what is dangerous," says former Surgeon General C. Everett Koop. The
truth is, Americans have never been healthier. Average life
expectancy has risen steadily for decades, and most cancer
death rates have remained stable or actually dropped.[1]

A while back an entire grape harvest was snatched off
American grocery shelves because two single grapes in an
East Coast market had been found to contain cyanide. The
two grapes made headline news, and from coast to coast
went up a mighty roar of indignation. I never heard what
hardships resulted for the South American grape growers. I
only know that recently a tiny newspaper article com-
mented that in the smoke of any single cigarette there is a
hundred times more cyanide than there was in those two
grapes.

Of course growers must be responsible to the public in
their use of insecticides. And of course all parents must be
responsible to their children to give them nourishing food.
But so must Christian families be responsible to God for
their attitude of restful faith in Him.

God says that He created foods

to be received with thanksgiving by those who believe and
know the truth. For everything God created is good, and
nothing is to be rejected if it is received with thanksgiving,
because it is consecrated by the word of God and prayer.
(1 Tim. 4:3–5)

*Christian family, give thanks for your food, and eat it together
with happy hearts.*

(The voices of fear are so loud everywhere around us, we
can resist giving up our most familiar, ensconced fears!
Romans 11 talks about *persisting* in unbelief.

---

1. Reprinted from "News from the World of Medicine," *Reader's Digest,*
November 1989, 26. An adaptation from © *The Washington Post* (7 May 1989,
A1), "Seeing Risk Everywhere" by Michael Spector. Used by permission.

A man went to a psychiatrist moaning, "Doctor, I'm dead."
"What?" said the doctor. "Listen, when you shave, sometimes you nick yourself and you bleed, right? Well, dead
men don't bleed."
To prove his point the doctor picked up a scalpel and
gently gave the man's chin a tiny nick and it bled.
"See, doc?" the fellow exclaimed, "dead men *do* bleed!")

3. *Christian parents may have an exaggerated, unhealthy
fear of the world and the devil.* And it's true, your little family
is tented smack in the middle of a huge battlefield! C. S.
Lewis said, "There is no neutral ground in the universe.
Every square inch, every second of time is claimed by God
and counterclaimed by the devil."
But to get a good perspective on what the Christian's
attitude about the world and the devil should be, take a
look at Matthew 13:24–30, Jesus' story about the wheat and
the weeds (tares).
The "tares," here, today we call darnel. It's a weed that
looks very much like wheat but it's very toxic. Of course our
natural instinct is to try to pull it out, but Jesus said no, you
might pull out some wheat, too. Leave it alone until the
harvest time.
But doesn't Jesus realize this stuff is poison? Shouldn't
Christians organize a big slash-and-burn party and try to
completely stamp all this stuff out?
Look, the time hasn't come. You try and eliminate the
darnel, and the same vandal who sneaked in and planted
it in the first place is still on the loose, and he'll just do it
again.

Christian parent, understand the nature of evil. Like any
weed, it's alive, it's multiplying, it's maturing. It has its own
dynamic; it tends not to wither but to grow toward full
maturity. From one sin planted in Genesis chapter 3, came a
huge harvest by chapter 6: "The Lord saw how great man's
wickedness on the earth had become, and that every incli-
nation of the thoughts of his heart was only evil all the
time" (6:5).
That's sin for you. One seed can produce a terrible crop.
It's true today, as well: evil is getting worse, it's maturing,

it's on its way to its full bumper crop of the last days (2 Timothy 3).

But so is the wheat! "Satan is alive and well on planet earth"—but so is God! Don't get any fixation on Satan; don't let him become some kind of hero in your children's eyes. Really, he's just a poor loser. And sin is actually stale, trite, dull.

On the other hand, think about the wheat. Righteousness doesn't seek to be noticed; it doesn't pay for many full-page ads; and yet its quiet influence is incredible.

"Jesus went about doing good"—and there was profound power in that. Goodness is dynamic, too! It's on the move; it, too, is growing toward its full bumper crop. Let your children know that sin is getting worse, but goodness is getting better.

Don't spend your time, then, clucking your tongue like some kind of grain inspector; often we're not smart enough, anyway, to discern motives and intents. God will take care of all that later.

But celebrate righteousness! Celebrate God, who will win! Let your kids know that as Christians they're victors! And deeply believe it yourself—in all your personal trials and in the worst of your family situations. Your trust in God will color everything.

Jacob's paternal favoritism of Joseph was not good. Joseph's brothers' schemes were not good. Potiphar was not good, prison was not good, famine was not good. But for Joseph and his family, God took a whole string of not-goods and turned them into good (Gen. 50:20; Rom. 8:28). And that is His consistent eternal way.

Then as you guide your family through all the traumas, *calmly trust Him.* Keep daily nourished in Scripture and prayer, and *calmly trust Him.* Fix your eyes on Jesus, and *calmly trust Him.*

"Our Lord God Almighty reigns" (Rev. 19:6).

"The Lord God is a sun and shield" (Ps. 84:11).

"Those who are with us are more than those who are with them" (2 Kings 6:16).

"Don't be afraid; just believe" (Mark 5:36).

Faith justifies the soul (Rom. 5:1). It purifies the heart (Acts 15:9). It overcomes the world (1 John 5:4).

In every family problem, as a gathered unit—hopefully including everyone—spell out your problems and needs to Jesus, and ask for help. And then—"Stop doubting and believe," as Jesus said (John 20:27). Hope in God for your situations! "Be of good cheer"—because you have Him!

Let me say it strongly: A doubting, worrying mother is a bad mother. She's modeling fear, not faith; and she'll produce worrying, anxious kids who have no idea that "God is our refuge and strength, an ever present help in trouble" (Ps. 46:1). This is of top importance, because "without faith it is impossible to please God" (Heb. 11:6). Your kids must get firmly planted in lives of trust.

How, then, parent, do you quit worrying? *You give up control.*

I can fuss and stew when I don't feel a sense of control over somebody or something. Then, again and again, I have to turn the control over to God—and immediately peace comes, and I rest.

Therapists tend to want to get you in control of a situation; that very need to control is the root of all paranoia. Give it up. Open your hands. Release it all to God. When you see your helplessness and ask God to help—only then is invisible machinery set in motion to start solving your problems.

I remember when Nels was just beginning to walk, one morning he stumbled into our swimming pool. Unfortunately, I was in the middle of a long phone conversation—and I never turned and saw him until he was floating, face down, unconscious, on the top of the water, like a quiet lily.

I ran for him, grabbed him out, got the water to start gushing out of him, saw him choke, vomit, revive and cry, bundled him in a blanket and rushed him to his doctor, held him in my arms as he got a penicillin shot, and brought him home for a long, long sleep in his crib with lots of blankets and a hot water bottle, to thaw his little body from marble blue-white to pink again.

By evening he was fine, and Ray babysat while I drove across town to teach a Bible class. Alone in the car for the first time, all my tensions and fears had an opportunity to surface. Oh, how long and loudly I bawled! I had to drive around a while and arrive late at the class to get it all out of my system. How physical the emotion of fear can become!

I remember at that time literally cupping my hands, as in my imagination I placed Nels in them and offered him to God. Ray has told me sometimes he's done the same thing with each of our children. We've released our fears and put our precious ones into His tender hands.

And would you believe it: Nels earned college money as a *lifeguard* and even ran his own little lifeguarding company for two summers!

Years ago Ginny and her eight-year-old Anna arrived as our new next-door neighbors. Ginny was in the process of divorcing, and she was panicky with fears that Scott would kidnap away their daughter. Only Psalm 91, repeated to Anna over and over every bedtime, restored Ginny's emotions enough for her to receive Christ as her Savior:

> . . . I will say of the Lord,"He is my refuge and my
>   fortress,
>   my God, in whom I will trust." . . .
> He will cover you with his feathers,
>   and under his wings you will find refuge. . . .
> You will not fear the terror of the night,
>   nor the arrow that flies by day. . . .
> No harm will befall you,
>   no disaster will come near your tent.

And it never did.

Do not be anxious about anything, but in everything, by prayer and petition, with thanksgiving, present your requests to God. And the peace of God, which transcends all

understanding, will guard your hearts and your minds in
Christ Jesus. (Phil. 4:6, 7)

> Worry is unnecessary.
>> The Lord is looking out for you and yours.
> Worry is futile.
>> It never solves the problem.
> Worry is harmful.
>> Doctors agree it causes many health problems.
> Worry is sin.
>> It doubts the wisdom and love and power of God.

Tony Melendez is a young Nicaraguan who was born
with no arms and one club foot. His story from poverty
and despair to concert tours and acclaim is told in his
moving book *A Gift of Hope*. The hope was given by his
mother:

> She believed that God had created me with something
> wonderful in mind, and she never let me forget it. When I
> grew discouraged, she said, "Trust God, Tony. He made
> you. He will take care of you. . . ."

> "Don't worry, Tony," Mom would reassure me again and
> again. "God has something wonderful in mind for you.
> Don't get impatient. . . . Trust Him and He will take care
> of you. You will see."[2]

Today, singing in concerts and playing his guitar with
his agile bare feet, Tony Melendez has received numerous
awards and honors, including a special commendation
from President Ronald Reagan. He has played for Pope
John Paul II. He has completed his first album, "Never
Be the Same," and his story is being featured on NBC
television.

One mother's gift to her son!

Give your family the same gift—unswerving trust in
God.

Do you believe in the sun even when it isn't shining?
Then believe in God even when He seems silent.

---

2. Tony Melendez, *A Gift of Hope* (New York: Harper and Row, 1989).

> Faith in God
>   sees the invisible,
>   believes the incredible,
>   and receives the impossible.

For your family life . . .
  "Grace, mercy and peace from God the Father
  and Christ Jesus our Lord" (2 Tim. 1:2).

  Grace for every step,
  Mercy for every stumble,
  Peace for every situation.

Think about it once more: Your little family is tented smack in the middle of a huge battlefield! How are you going to react? How are you going to lead your children to react?

With Almighty God protecting you and planning for you and providing for you and loving you, you have nothing to fear but fear itself.

> YOUR HOME HAS
> A MAGNIFICENT VIEW—
> IF YOU LOOK STRAIGHT UP

II. FAITH FOR THE CHILD

> *"Any parent knows that a newborn is just a loud voice at one end and no sense of responsibility at the other."*
>
> —Dr. Roy Fairchild

You have roughly twenty years to turn your new baby into a civilized human being, to lead him from immaturity to maturity, from fears to faith.

It's a big assignment.

Here comes a newborn into the world; talk about trauma! The womb was wonderful. It was an incredible all-provisional environment; this babe led an effortless existence. Stuart Emery has said it would take thousands of dollars a month to have an apartment in New York City comparable to the womb. It has twenty-four-hour security and twenty-four-hour room service. It has a constant level of temperature; it has peace, comfort, and safety.

Suddenly the tenant receives an eviction notice, and it wasn't his idea at all. Like it or not, he's bodily dumped out, even experiencing a drop in temperature of about 26 degrees. Talk about a "cold, cruel world"!

And he can't ever go back. No wonder he comes into the world crying—he's lost so much! It will be a long time before he may sense gains that really make up for his losses, opportunities which in the womb weren't possible.

Maybe as long as he lives, immaturity will keep him, even subconsciously, looking back with nostalgia—dreaming, fantasizing, trying to create for himself another womb. Or maybe he'll actually grow up, and he'll find the courage to look forward, be realistic, adjust, suffer, and achieve. He'll move from fears to faith!

**PORTRAIT:
JOSEPH: A YOUNG MAN
WE'D ALL LIKE TO HAVE RAISED**

Joseph got off to a shaky start. He came into the world after his father Jacob had had ten sons by three other women who couldn't stand each other, and his own mother Rachel couldn't get pregnant all those years and was almost hysterical with jealousy.

So when baby Joseph finally arrived he was the proof of Rachel's triumph, the adored extension of her own ego, hated by the other three women and all ten of their sons, and as obnoxious as the baby of the family can ever be.

(The fact that much later number twelve son would arrive didn't change Joseph's own status.)

Dr. Kevin Leman in *The Birth Order Book* talks about family "babies":

> Last borns carry the curse of not being taken very seriously, first by their families and then by the world. In fact, your typical last borns have a "burning desire to make an important contribution to the world." . . .
> Last borns are treated with ambivalence—coddled, cuddled and spoiled one minute, put down and made fun of the next. . . . We babies of the family grow up with an independent cockiness that helps cover all our self-doubt and confusion. We say to ourselves, "They wrote me off when I was little. . . . *I'll show them!*"[3]

But who could have ever pictured The Brat as someday prime minister of a world empire?

"Coddled, cuddled, spoiled":

> Israel loved Joseph more than any of his other sons, because he had been born to him in his old age, and he made a richly ornamented robe for him. (Gen. 37:3)

---

3. Kevin Leman, *The Birth Order Book* (Old Tappan, NJ: Revell, 1985), 135, 149.

"Put down and made fun of":

> When his brothers saw that their father loved him more
> than any of them, they hated him and could not speak a
> kind word to him. (v. 4)

Joseph's response to his brothers was tattling on them
(v. 2) and bragging in front of them (vv. 5–11). No wonder
they wanted to get rid of him!

When Joseph was lifted out of the cistern that day to be
sold to passing traders, all his fantasy-world had to be left
behind. Suddenly he was nobody's hothouse plant, the apple of nobody's eye. The essence of maturing, I think, must
be a willingness to live with how things are, rather than
how we wish they were. For the first time in his life, Joseph
could no longer dream and fantasize and take full advan-
tage of his little womblike world. It was time to choose reality: to look forward, be realistic, adjust, suffer, and achieve.

Little Last Born may have been thinking, "They wrote me
off: *I'll show them.*"

Even being sold to Potiphar, and into a second dysfunc-
tional family, didn't stop the process. Joseph's growing trust
in God (Gen. 39:9) matured his sense of reality; he understood his limits: "God has given me this, this, and this—but
not this. I can't take what He hasn't given" (Gen. 39:8, 9).
He had moved from fears to faith.

In prison as a result, he didn't look back, he didn't whim-
per over reduced status, he didn't ask why bad things happen to good people, he just went to work. As he had served
Potiphar, now he served the prison warden.

Joseph was grown up. He had once been parented; now
he did the parenting: he listened to the dreams and problems of others. It was the idea of, "Ask not what your country can do for you; ask what you can do for your country!"

And in time, this attitude put him in a position to do
exactly that, serve his entire country.

Joseph is a beautiful model of the maturing young person. Looking at him, you see what's needed between the
womb and adulthood: to train your kids to look not back

but forward, to lead them away from fantasizing to realism; to help them emerge from being cared for to caring, from being parented to parenting; to assist them in gaining the courage to be realistic, to adjust, suffer, and achieve.

In other words, *to lead them from fears to faith.* In the end a mature, successful Joseph could see the Big Picture and discern through good and through bad the quiet, persistent actions of a loving God. So he could say with total compassion to his chagrined older brothers,

> You intended to harm me, but God intended it for good, to accomplish what is now being done, the saving of many lives. (Gen. 50:20)

Joseph had come to see eternal truth—that God's reality is infinitely better than all our fantasies, that the losses from leaving the womb really do open up enormous opportunities for gain, that forward is truly better than back, that with God the best wine is always last.

What a joy, then—for you to learn to walk strongly forward with your Abba Father, your Lord God Almighty, the great Jehovah who guides you! And as your fears dissolve into faith, keep your children close by you—so that before long theirs will do the same.

NOW WORK INTO YOUR LIFE WHAT YOU'VE BEEN READING.

I. FAITH FOR THE PARENTS

1. Don't rush on to the next chapter until you've answered a crucial question:
Are you basically living by fears or by faith?
Write down things you're afraid of. (In a group, allow some quiet time for this, and then overcome some momentary fears enough to read your lists to each other!)

2a. Joshua 1:6–9 says that *faithful Bible reading* can produce a certain result. What is it (vv. 6, 7, 9)? How does the rest of the book of Joshua indicate that Israelite history profited from the obedience of one man, Joshua?

2b. Second Chronicles 15:1–15 says that in a wicked society, *Spirit-filled preaching* can produce a certain result. What is it (v. 8)? And what was the effect here on all the Israelites because of the obedience of one man, Asa?

2c. How can it make a difference in your own world if you're a person of faith and courage?

3. Memorize 1 Corinthians 16:13.

4. Read 1 Samuel 29:6 to see that even if you're in a terrible situation, you can encourage your own heart in God. Tell Him in prayer that you will do this.

II. FAITH FOR THE CHILDREN

1. The Bible says that fearing the Lord is to be our one positive, happy, wholesome fear. What can you do to instill this one fear in your children?
Read Proverbs 14:26. Can you think of specific

ways to build your children's sense of security in God? See also Isaiah 54:13.

2. You long to establish (or else continue) a godly line of descendants, as described in Psalm 112:1, 2.

Read verses 6–8, and pray that each of your children, by name, will become this. Don't rush your praying. Don't go on to the ninth Drastic Do until you feel you've made headway in your heart about this matter of your and your family's putting off fears and putting on faith.

And as you wait before Him, envision each of your children, one at a time, becoming strong, faithful men and women of God. Starting today, begin a daily prayer habit of seeking God's promises in His Word for your children, and then holding these promises back up to Him in continuous, persistent prayer. See Luke 11:5–10 and Luke 18:1–7.

Learn to Cocoon

> *"He strengthens the bars of your gates and blesses your people within you"*
> —Psalm 147:13

> *"The best way to keep children home is to make the home atmosphere pleasant —and let the air out of the tires."*
> —Dorothy Parker[1]

Cocooning is in. It's the new term for an old occupation—being at home! Somewhere back in 1989 somebody was wandering the streets and couldn't think of anything to do, and he thought, "Hey, I could go home." It seemed like a really far-out, outrageous thing to do, but he tried it. And the idea's been catching on ever since.

I heard about a gal who said she didn't know where her husband was every night. Recently one night she stayed home—and there he was!

Colonel Sanders' business has never been so hot. In fact, suddenly at any fast food place they're hardly asking, "Here or to go?" The big thing is to go—home. In America, at least, restaurants mail out their menus, and they promise dinner delivered to your home within fifty-nine minutes. Movies are to rent and take home.

---

1. *Peter's Quotations* (New York: Bantam, 1977), 77.

Well, as long as you're home you could play patty cake with the baby, or "so big," or peekaboo, or "This little piggy went to market."

With a little older one you could do "Here's a church, here's a steeple" with your fingers. Or make a cat's cradle with string. Or lie on your tummies on the floor and play Parcheesi or Old Maid or dominoes or jacksticks or marbles.

With older ones you could break out the card table and have a vicious game of Monopoly or Trivial Pursuit or Uno. If you got hungry you could pile sandwiches together and make cocoa.

You could mark the children's heights on a doorjamb with a book and a pencil.

You could get out the photo album and paste in 947 loose snapshots waiting in a shoe box. You could put up the projector and see slides or movies of the "old days," or see the videos. You could bring the baby books up to date.

You could make up stories, breaking them off at a high point, and the next person has to go on from there.

You could go outside and toss the football or throw the Frisbee or jump rope or play hopscotch or fly kites. Or make a snowman.

The possibilities are endless.

I read an article recently about summer camps. (Incidentally, "a lot of parents pack up their troubles and send them off to summer camp!") But this article exhorted, "Sending your children away to camp teaches them flexibility." I'm not opposed to camps, but I have yet to see a child who needs flexibility. *Old* people need flexibility. Kids need security! They need *a place.* They need *the same people.* They need to *do the same things over and over* in that place, not to be sent somewhere else. They need patterns, habits, rhythms that build the foundation of comfortableness and trust.

Said Robert Frost, "Home is the place where, when you have to go there, they have to take you in."

Better than that,
   "The house of the righteous stands firm" (Prov. 12:7).

"The Lord's curse is on the house of the wicked,
   but he blesses the home of the righteous" (Prov. 3:32).

In all the little daily patterns of the home—the laundry going into the same hamper, the sweaters into the same drawer, the hair getting washed and the shoes polished on Saturday nights—God is at work. He delights to glorify Himself in the commonplace. He chooses the lowly things of this world, even the despised things, to prevail over the seemingly powerful (1 Cor. 1:28). He fills ordinary water containers with His mysterious wine. He fills clay jars with treasures. He makes our little daily chores channels of His grace.
   And, says Gloria Gaither,

> Children are learners. They learn everywhere. They learn sitting down and standing up. They learn wide awake and half asleep. They take in knowledge through their eyes, ears, noses, taste buds, fingers, feet, and skin. They learn while parents are teaching, and they learn while parents hope they're not teaching. Children learn from joy, they learn from pain. They learn from hot, cold, work, play, comfort and discomfort.
>   Sometimes we adults associate learning [only] with books. . . . But when the books are closed and the lessons are over, children go on learning. No knobs turn off their little minds. . . . They go on learning, watching me, seeing how I handle problems, sensing my unguarded reactions, picking up the "vibes" of our home."[2]

You can have endless variety in the way you put together your family life, but whatever you do, you can't omit two disciplines and thrive. These two are to be your bedrock, regular, ceaseless, foundational home activities of the drastic new lifestyle.

---

   2. Gloria Gaither, "Those Teachable Moments," *Moody Monthly* Magazine, Sept. 1978, 91–92.

TWO DRASTIC DISCIPLINES FOR
YOUR COCOONING

One: At least once a day sit down and eat together.

"Now when the even was come, [Jesus] sat down with the twelve" (Matt. 26:20, KJV).

No one was busier than Christ was—but this was His appointment, to which He was committed.

"The Lord Jesus, on the night he was betrayed, took bread . . ." (1 Cor. 11:23).

He sat down with Judas who would betray Him, and with Peter who would deny Him. . . . He sat down.

Eating together is a sacred thing, a ritual of commitment to each other. It says loud and clear, without any words, "We belong to each other." The family table should be a central spot of the home; you have many beds but only one board.

> Blessed are all who fear the Lord,
>   who walk in his ways. . . .
> Your wife will be like a fruitful vine
>   within your house;
> your sons will be like olive shoots
>   around your table. (Ps. 128:1, 3)

The ritual of the table is to be faithfully observed.

Within an hour or two before, nobody microwaves a pizza. They must come hungry.

The TV is off. (Forty percent of American families watch television while they eat! Unless some history-changing world event is taking place, no. No. No, no, no. Never again until the children are out of the nest. Then the rules can change to suit yourselves—but even then, watch the need for communication.)

1. Everyone gathers promptly at the appointed hour. Hopefully Mother gets seated by a male member of the family. (I usually do at least Thanksgiving and Christmas.) (To this day John is never allowed to seat his sister-in-law Sherry. He'd land her on the floor.)

2. Then comes the blessing—hopefully by Father or whomever Father appoints. Otherwise Mother instigates it.

3. Mother always takes the first bite. (When our kids are home they have their forks poised, heads bent over for action, screaming at me, "Take a bite! Take a bite!")

4. You sit up. You look each other in the eye. You eat slowly. You talk. (This one's a toughie, because they have to be taught that meals are for fellowship as well as food. They'll want to just put their heads down and shovel it in. Even show them how to hold their knives and forks and to keep their free hand in their lap; it could make a difference in their careers. One time Ray didn't hire a man because his table manners were so bad; he figured they were an indication of the rest of his living.)

5. You pass what's in front of you. You offer seconds. Manners develop thoughtfulness, concern for others.

6. You wait between courses till all are through before you take off plates or begin a new course. If you're feeling fancy, no stacking at the table.

7. Hopefully you have fun! Food digests better with laughter.

8. No one leaves the table before Mother does. If they must, they ask her if they may be excused.

Sounds complicated? Look, any pig can go to a trough and satisfy himself. You're not raising pigs but people.

By the way, don't get too impressed with the Ortlunds' eating habits. My influence means so little that when we get together—even though we observe most of the above rules—the males, now in their maturity, often have raucous burping contests, or open wide their full mouths to display everything. Especially in front of the females. And they consistently get the same reaction—the females scream, "Oh, gross, gross!"

During Ray's twenty years at Lake Avenue Congregational Church when the children were all in the nest, his evenings got fuller and fuller. In those days, we realized that dinner was too rushed to be the central family meal.

So breakfast became traditionally the Big One, and we gave it over an hour. No matter what I threw together in the evening, breakfasts were Big Deal. I might fix any of these:

Hot cereal

French toast

Baked corned beef hash with eggs

Other egg dishes

Waffles with different toppings

Broiled fish with broiled tomato halves

Toasted bacon sandwiches

Pancakes

Fried grits or cornmeal mush with syrup

Creamed chipped beef on biscuits

Ham and fried potatoes.

The fruits were varied: juices or melons or hot baked apples or broiled grapefruit halves with honey or either pineapple sticks or strawberries with powdered sugar. . . .
The breads were varied: toast or sweet rolls or muffins or hot biscuits or English muffins or rusks. . . .
The drinks were varied: coffee, cocoa, milk. . . .

It was then that we had family devotions and shared what was going on in our lives and got prayed for.

They told what things were done along the way, and
. . . [Jesus] was known of them in breaking of bread. (Luke 24:35, KJV)

The Missouri Synod Lutherans have composed a wonderful litany which would be a great thing for a family to memorize and say together at the end of every dinner, holding hands:

God made us a family.
We need one another.

> We love one another.
> We forgive one another.
> We work together.
> We play together.
> We worship together.
> Together we use God's Word.
> Together we grow in Christ.
> Together we love all men.
> Together we serve our God.
> Together we hope for heaven.
> These are our hopes and ideals;
> Help us to attain them, O God;
> Through Jesus Christ our Lord, Amen.[3]

I could see memorizing and saying in unison the first four lines when your children are very small, adding the next three lines to total seven when they get bigger, and adding the next four to total eleven still later. . . .

Before long it would certainly become pure routine, and yet it would be, even subconsciously, a powerful affirmation of your family's unity and specialness under God. And it would shape their ideals later for raising their own families.

* * * * *

The second drastic discipline for your cocooning:
Once a day have family worship.

You say your family is full of stepparents and stepchildren and castoffs and misfits and also-rans? *"The family that prays together stays together."* Try it. Have patience—and yet before long the mellowing and meshing will begin to happen.

You only have one stretch of time—a very few years, really—to help them understand what in life is most important. *You're teaching values.*

When you reward your children for physical or intellectual or social accomplishments and not for Christian

---

3. "The Christian Family Standard" adopted by the Family Life Committee of the Lutheran Church, Missouri Synod. Quoted by Oscar Feucht in *Helping Families through the Church* (Saint Louis, MO: Concordia, 1957).

accomplishments, they're getting a system of false values. Again, if you feed them nourishing food for their bodies and you don't feed them the Word and prayer and fellowship for their spirits, they're getting a monstrously false impression.

But "once a day"? Doesn't that seem too drastic? Impossible?

They can't be fed spiritually just once a week in church any more than they could get fed physically only once a week. *You're teaching values*—what's important on a scale of one to ten—by what you don't do as well as by what you do. Says the Lord,

> Do not let this Book of the Law depart from your mouth; meditate on it day and night, so that you may be careful to do everything written in it. Then you will be prosperous and successful. (Josh. 1:8)

> Day after day . . . Ezra read from the Book of the Law of God [to the people]. (Neh. 8:18)

> The Bereans were of more noble character . . . for they . . . examined the Scriptures every day. (Acts 17:11)

"Biblical truth," writes Dr. Carl Henry, "transcultural as it is, proclaims the gospel to a generation that is intellectually uncapped, morally unzipped, and volitionally uncurbed"![4] Says Dr. Donald Bloesch,

> If anything characterizes modern Protestantism, it is the absence of spiritual disciplines or spiritual exercises. Yet such disciplines form the core of the life of devotion. It is not an exaggeration to state that this is the lost dimension of modern Protestantism.[5]

Can you—for your family—recover the lost? Yes, you can, but you haven't a minute to lose. Start reading God's Word and praying with your kids every day. This may be so

4. "The Road to Eternity," *Christianity Today*, July 17, 1981, 32.
5. Donald G. Bloesch, *The Crisis of Piety* (Grand Rapids, MI: Eerdmans, 1968), 63.

opposed to, and opposite from, their present culture that it would seem a truly drastic thing to do—especially if your children are getting bigger and this hasn't been their habit.

What can we say?

If this world's culture is an avalanche sliding toward hell, and it is; and you don't want your own precious children to go with it, and you don't—

Then apologize for your delay, roll up your sleeves, use all your strength, and literally snatch them out of the current mind-set and leap in the opposite direction—for that solid Rock!

```
          PORTRAIT:
        THE PETERS FAMILY
```

Jon and Sallie Peters have three children, all in the wiggly, messy stage. They live in one of those comfy early-American homes with lots of baskets and braided rugs and rocking chairs. They're into health foods and aerobics and Scrabble after the kids are in bed.

Jon's job takes him traveling usually over two nights a week. When he's home he leads the family in devotions; when he's gone, Sallie takes over.

Jon's theory is "short children, short devotions; longer children, longer devotions." So theirs are still pretty short—maybe five to ten minutes.

Sometimes they read a little bit of Scripture from *The Living Bible.* (Recently some bits have been

Psalm 95:5, 6

Proverbs 20:11

Psalm 92:1, 2

1 John 4:11

Proverbs 20:12.)

Sometimes they tell a Bible story. Lately they've told about—but not read—Daniel eating good food (Dan. 1:3–16); Jesus loving to have little children around Him (Matt. 19:13–15); God making the earth and everything in it—people, too (Gen. 1); and Philip telling a man about Jesus (Acts 8:35).

Sometimes they memorize a verse together. Some of these have been—

"I will trust and not be afraid" (Isa. 12:2) and
"Children, obey your parents" (Eph. 6:1).

(Jeffrey, two, just sits and looks, wide-eyed, with his thumb in his mouth.)

Sometimes Jon asks for a "testimony"—how Jesus has helped one of them that day.

Almost always they sing at least one song together, often action songs that require standing up and sitting down. (Jeffrey just sits and looks, wide-eyed, with his thumb in his mouth.)

Then they have prayer. They fold their hands and bow their heads and shut their eyes, and sometimes Jon prays and sometimes Sallie prays and sometimes one of the older kiddies gets prodded into praying.

Jon says later he'll start shifting to the New International Version and read a little longer passages, stopping to explain words or ask questions. They'll do a little more memorizing. Eventually he hopes they'll memorize the names of the books of the Bible and have races looking up verses, with prizes.

He has also stashed away Kenneth Taylor's *Devotions for the Children's Hour* (Moody Press) and Donald Grey Barnhouse's *Teaching the Word of Truth.* The latter is a systematized study of doctrine with stick-men illustrations.

(We hope that when Jon does all these wonderful things, Jeffrey won't be sitting there, wide-eyed, with his thumb in his mouth.)

And all this isn't only for the children. It brings the two of you close in an important daily commitment together before the Lord.

What if one spouse isn't a believer, or simply can't or won't take part? Or what if you're on your own, raising your family as a single parent? Still you can gather together whomever you have, or whoever will come, daily before Him. In effect you'll be saying, "Here am I, and the children the Lord has given me" (Isa. 8:18).

Learn to cocoon: Eat together, worship together. In these days those practices are drastic!

Make a *family* out of your family.

NOW WORK INTO YOUR LIFE
WHAT YOU'VE BEEN READING.

1. The smell of baked cookies permeating the house when Dad or the kids come home is probably mostly gone, but what *really* draws family members back to the nest?

    a. If your home has two parents, make a list of what draws—or would draw—*her* back.

    Then make a list of what draws—or would draw—*him* back.

    Now rate on a scale of one to ten whether those warm, nice things are strongly present, sometimes present, mostly lacking, totally absent. What can you do to correct or improve your home's drawing power for your spouse?

    b. List what draws, or would draw, the kids back. Do you see some drastic new plans for action?

2. Proverbs 27:8 is such a sad, pathetic verse! And straying children are just as tragic, even if they're just chronically roaming "mall orphans." God loves homes! He knows the stabilizing, securing effect it has on His people to have a *place*.

Read carefully Isaiah 32:17, 18, a prophecy of what happens when the Holy Spirit comes upon His people. Pray that your home may become, or continue to be, this kind of center—a center for righteousness, peace, quiet, and confidence for every person under your roof.

Get Control of Your Finances

> *Workers earn it,*
> *Spendthrifts burn it,*
> *Bankers lend it,*
> *Women spend it,*
> *Forgers fake it,*
> *Taxes take it,*
> *Dying leave it,*
> *Heirs receive it,*
> *Thrifty save it,*
> *Misers crave it,*
> *Robbers seize it,*
> *Rich increase it,*
> *Gamblers lose it. . . .*
> *I could use it.* [1]

Are you relating? If you're typical—even a typical Christian—you're in poor financial health. You've got get-rich-quick dreams in your head, you're into fudging (lying) in financial matters, or you have investment worries or overdue bills.

Eighty percent of all Christian families are either overspending now or are still suffering from past overspending!

---

1. Richard Armor, *Going Like Sixty: A Lighthearted Look at the Later Years* (New York: McGraw-Hill, 1974), 77–78.

In that sense they're definitely "worldly": they've joined the mind-set and lifestyle of the society around them.
    Says Martha Bolton,

> Every family ought to have a budget—a list that shows exactly what you'll need to borrow from American Express to pay off your VISA card so you can use it to charge your MasterCard payment so you'll be below limit and can use that to charge your Discovery and Dining Club payments."[2]

And that's about the way we operate!
    If you're this average Christian family, you need to make some drastic revisions in your money handling. You need to take control again, to gather it together and channel it according to a good plan.
    If you're typical you need drastic new ways to earn, spend, save, and give. Let's talk about each of those.

1. Get drastic new wisdom for earning your money.
    Ralph Waldo Emerson said it right: "Money often costs too much!"
    Jesus said, "Do not work for food that spoils, but for food that endures to eternal life" (John 6:27). And another time He said, "Look at the birds of the air; they do not sow or reap or store away in barns, and yet your heavenly Father feeds them. Are you not much more valuable than they?" (Matt. 6:26).
    Is He saying, "Quit working and sit around"? No, 2 Thessalonians 3 says it's not good to be idle.
    But *even as you work, understand where your supply comes from: your heavenly Father. And if you are not able to work, keep on understanding where your supply comes from: your heavenly Father.*

    Your job is not your source of supply, your Father is. That's a drastic concept. Wash the world's concepts right out of your head, and believe the word of your Abba Father, Almighty God!

---

2. Martha Bolton, *If Mr. Clean Calls, Tell Him I'm Not In* (Ventura, CA: 1989), 43.

Then if you need *more* money, the answer isn't necessarily for more people in the family to work, or to work harder or longer; the need is to look to your Source: "Give us this day our daily bread."

Maybe He's created the shortfall to teach you dependence and prayer. What's He saying to you? What are you learning? . . . Keep your attention on the divine Distributor.

> The eyes of all look to you,
>   and you give them their food at the proper time.
> You open your hand
>   and satisfy the desires of every living thing. (Ps. 145:15, 16)

Never, never does He mean for you to exhaust yourself "like the heathen" (Matt. 6:32)—like all those orphans!

Yuppies hyperaggressive to "be millionaires by thirty" are doing to themselves physiologically exactly what Columbia River salmon do, fighting their way upstream. The salmon, also, are "climbing the ladder," and they make it—and then die of cardiovascular exhaustion. Learning to be content (see Ps. 131) will literally heal your heart.

> It is senseless for you to work so hard from early morning until late at night, fearing you will starve to death; for God wants his loved ones to get their proper rest. (Ps. 127:5, TLB)

> He gives food to those who trust him; he never forgets his promises. (Ps. 111:5, TLB)

Ask Him, because He's trying to teach you to pray. But also *expect Him* to take care of you. If you truly believe that the Lord is your Shepherd, then you shall not want.

If you're in a situation where your job hurts your family and yet seems indispensable, and what I'm advising sounds too totally drastic—stop, look, and listen. Are there reservations in your heart? Are you saying, "Yes, I want to live God's way, but there's no way we could get along with less money"?

Jesus put it right to us when He said, "You cannot serve both God and Money" (Matt. 6:24). The bottom line is, you choose to depend on your money, or you choose to depend on Him.

Tottie Ellis, Vice President of Eagle Forum, guesting an editorial column recently for a secular newspaper, wrote this:

> Money may buy a house but it won't buy a home. It may buy acquaintances but it won't buy friendship. Money can hire somebody to watch the children, but it cannot buy nurturing.
>
> We worship at the altar of objects. The material is elevated to a place of absolute value, causing the family to lose vitality. *We've become more devoted to possessions than to the children!* [italics mine]
>
> . . . America is in danger of losing its way. . . . Materialism is a monster which is loose in our nation and attacking our families. . . . You can have the family without society, but not society without the family. . . .[3]

May God give you, reader, drastic new wisdom, clarity, insight for your earning money, and may He give you the courage, as well, to obey that wisdom.

PORTRAIT:
BOB AND BRENDA

Bob Ortlund is our nephew. Age thirty-eight, Bob is another typical Ortlund, with a blond, Swedish-American look; he could be one of our own kids. What you notice about him right away is that he's medium framed but incredibly muscular. As a child Bob was small, quiet, and asthmatic. Then through his high school and college days, the Lord "grew" him in every dimension. And he developed both a body and a spirit of solid steel.

---

3. *USA Today,* 30 August, 1989, 8A.

All his adult life Bob has been a forest-fire fighter. He has watched America dry out: he used to be away from his home and family fighting fires three months of the year; now it averages six, but has been up to nine. He and his buddies get airlifted all over the western United States, to do what must be one of the world's dirtiest, most exhausting, and most dangerous jobs—and sometimes on little food and sleep for many days, and sometimes losing his friends. The pain of it all, especially being away from his family for long stretches, has caused a stomach ulcer.

"Still," his wife Brenda tells me, "the ulcer's much better now. The Lord wonderfully gave him a better job as a Fire Management Officer; he still does fire fighting but it's part administration, too, so even during fire season now he's not gone so constantly."

Brenda is like Bob: strong and quiet and unflappable. She stays at home in their small town in the mountains of Arizona with Sarah, nine; David, six; and Breanna, eighteen months. She feels a lot of pressure from other people to get a job and add to Bob's modest salary.

Brenda says to me, "The Lord is so wonderful. I pray that He'll honor our obedience in the lifestyle we've chosen, and He does: I find things on sale really often—like half price for the kids' things! The quality is great, but the price is 'way down. That's only the Lord."

And it will blow you away when I tell you how well they're doing in ownership of this world's goods—but I'll save that for later.

2. Get drastic new wisdom for spending your money.

The spirit of the world is discontent and greed. I'm all for free enterprise—but the fact is, the free enterprise system, overused, can keep you so dissatisfied that you buy and buy and buy.

Now there's nothing basically wrong with living comfortably and dressing well and driving a nice car. It depends on the price! If they came at the cost of too much debt, or disagreeing over whether to buy or not to buy, or simply out of spirit of discontent; or if desire for them makes us cut back on saving or giving, or makes us take on too many jobs to pay for them—then, for us, at this time, they're wrong.

> Coveting is material inebriation. It's an addiction to things that don't last and a craving for things that don't really matter. It forces us to depend on tomorrow to bring us the happiness that today couldn't supply."[4]

> A greedy man brings trouble to his family. (Prov. 15:27)

> Keep your lives free from the love of money and be content with what you have. (Heb. 13:5)

As parents, as a family, *discipline your desires.* Otherwise, four things will happen:

(1) Your family life will have an atmosphere of being cheated, or being incomplete.

(2) You'll place unbearable strain on your marriage. If either spouse is pressured by the other to supply more than he or she can supply, there will be a deep sense of inadequacy and failure.

(3) You'll compound stress in your children. "Environment, where the best is always in the future," says Tim Kimmel, "breeds an attitude that makes the present look cheap."[5]

(4) You will play into the hands of the powers of this world system that want to control you. Your chronic borrowing from them to "keep up" makes you their servant and makes them your lords.

"The rich rule over the poor, and the borrower is servant to the lender" (Prov. 22:7).

Which brings us to your third need for wisdom:
3. *Get drastic new wisdom for saving your money.*

If you'll start today saving $10 a week at 8 percent interest, compounded daily, in five years you'll have $3,194. In

---

4. From *Little House on the Freeway* (Portland, OR: Multnomah Press, 1987) as quoted in *Focus on the Family* Magazine, Feb. 1988, 3.
5. Ibid., 3.

ten years you'll have $7,960; in twenty, $25,673. And in thirty years of faithfully stashing away that modest little ten dollars a week, you'll have $65,092!

Says the Lord in Proverbs 13:11,

Dishonest money dwindles away,
but he who gathers money little by little makes it grow.

When you buy something on credit you not only lose the price of the merchandise but the interest on the loan as well—and that interest can be very high.

When you save for it in advance and pay cash, you've been paying *yourself* as that money waited, accumulating in the bank. Then you have the purchase and a reward for yourself as well!

Long ago Ben Franklin said, "He that can have patience can have what he will."

So here is a drastic financial discipline (perhaps excluding your home and, in early years, your car) which will put you light years ahead: "Pay as you go, or don't go."

PORTRAIT, CONTINUED

I want to tell you more about Bob and Brenda Ortlund's money handling.

When they got married they had literally no money. Brenda was in the middle of her senior year of college, and they got married on her spring break. Bob had finished college and had his first full-time job—with the Forest Service, marking timber. They lived in Flagstaff, a good-sized city in the Arizona mountains, where Brenda's school was.

With her bachelor's degree in hand, Brenda's heart's desire was graduate work in the same university. Bob tried to find work in the city, but nothing opened up. Meanwhile the Forest Service offered him a firefighting job: he'd be stationed in Young—population 400!—which was quite a distance away from school and deeper into the mountains.

Should they live apart except for weekends? They both agreed it wouldn't be good for their marriage. So Brenda put away her graduate dreams, and they moved to Young. From there she often traveled on one-day trips to distant schools, either as a speech therapist or as a substitute teacher.

Both were working and saving. . . .

Eventually they could buy a small trailer and a little piece of ground. They rejoiced over getting a "toehold" in some equity! Other good things were happening, too. They got involved in the little local church and made dear friends, and baby Sarah was born. After that Brenda worked only occasionally, taking Sarah along. Now there was much less income, a third mouth to feed—and Bob and Brenda decided to start tithing!

Laughing, Brenda says that once they started, they kept tithing no matter what. All the bills kept getting paid, and they didn't know if they missed a month if that would change. . . .

Life had its tough times. Bob was offered a better fire-fighting job and a move to Payson, a larger town, but when they were ready to sell their trailer—imagine the irony—it caught fire and burned! Salvaging what money they could in selling "as is," with their drastically shrunken equity they bought a place in Payson.

It was a tiny house with two bedrooms. Bob often says he doesn't know how his income stretched in those years, but they kept adding an extra twenty-dollar payment to the principal whenever they could. They both were willing to sacrifice to whittle down their debt. And even with the arrival of baby David, eventually they owned their little home free and clear.

A friend showed them a piece of ground they could buy. "Why don't you build?" he said. Even owning the lot, they didn't know when they'd be able to put a house on it—but they were outgrowing the little one, so they kept saving. Bob gets a lot of overtime pay during fire season, so each fall they'd add a big lump.

In three years they were ready to build: a wonderful two-story home on a hillside, with large rooms and four bedrooms. They built it all at once, with Bob and Brenda, not knowledgeable in construction, contributing what labor they could.

"At least to us, our home is so beautiful," these two say, who are still only thirty-eight years old! We've tried to be faithful, but it's really just the Lord. We feel so thankful. He's been so good to us."

4. Get drastic new wisdom for giving your money.

When you've restrained yourself from overspending and you've systematically saved, you will always have, to give. What a relief—to be on top of it instead of always under! To live financially on the offense, not the defense!

And what fun! Remember "the words the Lord Jesus himself said: 'It is more blessed to give than to receive'" (Acts 20:35).

Here's how God lays it out for you:

Do not show ill will toward your needy brother and give him nothing. He may then appeal to the Lord against you, and you will be found guilty of sin. Give generously to him and do so without a grudging heart; then because of this the Lord your God will bless you in all your work and in everything you put your hand to. (Deut. 15:9–10)

There will always be poor in the land. Therefore I command you to be openhanded toward your brothers and toward the poor and needy in your land. (Deut. 15:11)

This isn't being "liberal" or "conservative," this is God's Word. And my purpose here isn't to consider what part the government should play, but what you as a family should do.

In America, at least (and many places elsewhere), the Great Divide between rich and poor has been widening, in part because the rich have been close-fisted. Look what's been happening:

In 1969 the richest 5 percent of Americans owned 15.6 percent of America's wealth.

In 1979 they owned 15.8 percent of it.
In 1987 they owned 16.9 percent of it![6]
If you're in this category, here's what God says:

Command those who are rich in this present world not
to be arrogant nor to put their hope in wealth, which is so
uncertain, but to put their hope in God, who richly pro-
vides us with everything for our enjoyment.
Command them to do good, to be rich in good deeds,
and to be generous and willing to share. In this way they
will lay up treasure for themselves as a firm foundation for
the coming age, so that they may take hold of the life that is
truly life. (1 Tim. 6:17–19)

If you say you're just "middle class"—compared with
much of the world you're truly rich, and these words apply
also to you. If you feel you're struggling, it may be partly
because you live in an area of the world where the standards and expectations are always rising, and it's easy to
jump on the bandwagon of the discontented, the hyped, the
Type A's, the greedy, the exhausted.
The world is full of people so busy stretching for the
brass ring that they forget to enjoy the merry-go-round.
Says the Lord,

Good will come to him who is generous and lends freely.
. . .
He has scattered abroad his gifts to the poor,
    his righteousness endures forever;
    his horn will be lifted high in honor. (Ps. 112:5, 9)

But—"If a man shuts his ears to the cry of the poor," God
says, "he too will cry out and not be answered" (Prov. 21:13).

Obviously we've been shutting our ears to their cry, because the poor have been getting poorer.
In America, in 1969 the poorest 20 percent of the people
owned only 5.6 percent of the nation's wealth.
In 1979 they owned 5.2 percent of it.

------

6. *Business Week*, Sept. 1989, 178.

In 1987 they owned only 4.6 percent of it![7]
Realistically, this translates into growing homelessness, disintegrating housing, more sickness without medical care, more dropping out of school, deeper loss of hope, and ever-stronger temptations to stealing and drugs.

And if this distresses you—in places of galloping inflation like Brazil and Argentina, or in famine areas like Sudan and Ethiopia, the misery of the poor is even greater.

Open your heart and your wallet! Part of repentance and renewal in the Christian family should be a drastic rebirth of a sense of responsibility toward the poor. One "discipline of the home" should be regular, ongoing giving to ease their suffering.

To paraphrase Proverbs 14:21—

> The family which despises its neighbor sins,
> but blessed is the one which is kind to the needy.

And a similar paraphrase of Proverbs 22:9—

> A generous family will themselves be blessed,
> for they share their food with the poor.

One of your disciplines of the home should be planned giving. To your church and other Christian efforts, of course.

But also, have a jar on the breakfast table where both adults and children can drop in bills or coins for the poor. Take out of it when people you know are legitimately hurting for money. And when it's full, all together pray over that money and the poor people who will receive it, and then send it on its way to rescue missions, Salvation Army, World Vision, or wherever, and throw in a generous check besides. Then start filling the jar again.

> He who is kind to the poor lends to the Lord,
> and he will reward him for what he has done.
> (Prov. 19:17)

---

7. Ibid., 178.

NOW WORK INTO YOUR LIFE
WHAT YOU'VE BEEN READING.

1. Jesus had much to say about money. Prayerfully read Matthew 6:19–34, and let Him teach you.
2. Assess where you're strong, where you're weak in

    a. Earning,
    b. Spending,
    c. Saving,
    d. Giving.

Can you frankly guess why you're weak in any of these areas? Does it go back to fears versus faith? Is the bottom line a decision regarding Matthew 6:24?

Maybe it's time to make a fresh, full commitment to the Lord. (On your knees?) If you're in a group, you may want to do this as well.

3. First comes decision, then action. Before you go on to the next chapter, take some drastic new steps to take back control of your money—"to gather it together and channel it according to a good plan." If you have a spouse, do this together; pray that your hearts will be agreed. If necessary make an appointment with a financial advisor—perhaps even a godly couple in your church with a good track record. Would it be good to be accountable to them for a while, to get off to a good start?

"[You can be] confident of this, that he who began a good work in you will carry it on to completion until the day of Christ Jesus."
—Philippians 1:6

Even what He has begun to work in your family!

He's very diligent about it. Said Jesus, "My Father is always at his work" (John 5:17).

The only thing is, He is spirit, and you can't literally watch Him do it, and you can't hear Him breathing hard. . . . But He is working.

And working.

And working.

God is at work in everything. In everything.

All the time.

When a couple, say, leaves home for the office on any given morning, they're probably only aware of their own work, and not conscious—or barely conscious—of God's. But He is very busy. . . .

When [they] rush outside, their shoes scuff through the outer layers of atoms in the carpet, like Dr. Zhivago and Lara trudging through snowdrifts, sending sheets of ions flying like powder. The couple receives a 400-volt electrical charge in the process, but that discharges the moment they touch the metal doorknob. The carpet, left behind, has no such outlet. For half an hour their electrostatic footprints will remain clearly in place. With special equipment that can photograph heat images, the path would show a dim blue-green.

The bustle of the humans' departure causes other changes, as well. On a cold day, some of the vapor from water that evaporated up from all the hand washing, teeth cleaning and showering—possibly five pounds of it on the average busy morning—will have to come down. Part of the water will soak into the wooden floorboards and make them swell. Other water will cling to the walls.

The empty house does not sit still. For one thing, sunlight is banging against the window glass, and some rays are squishing through and piling up. They heat the dining-room table, splitting formaldehyde loose from the varnish, and also warm up the carpet fibers and the pockets of air between them, producing a slow-motion, Medusa-like writhing. This starts air currents rising.

Where the sunlight hits the walls, it causes color-giving particles floating in the paint to vibrate like pinball flippers on the loose. Much of the radiation carries through to the underlying brick or wood or concrete. This stretches the material in all directions, yanks it up, pulls on every nail and screw in the wall and pushes the roof upward. The whole house begins to stretch. By the time the couple comes home, the house will be several centimeters larger, but when night falls it will sag again.

Even in rooms where there is no direct sunlight, there are other curious goings-on. Sweaters stacked in drawers leach molecules into one another, while hangers in the closet, sagging from the weight of clothes, emit an ultra-low-frequency groan.[1]

Who would have thought it? Who could have imagined?
And all this physical activity is typical of a million other ways, as well, that God is silently working.

---

1. From *The Secret House* copyright © 1986 by David Bodanis. Reprinted by permission of Simon & Schuster, Inc. Also reprinted with permission from the February 1987 *Reader's Digest.*

And your family—whatever the combination of humans under your roof—is a mystery, a marvel, a wonder. God has put you together, and things are happening in you and between you, from day to day, from moment to moment, of which you're totally unaware.

His movements are constant, but they're often subdued, delicate, even invisible. Mostly, you can only realize what He's been up to, in you and your family, in retrospect, as you look back. You have to read God's work in your life like Hebrew: backward.

But imperceptibly He's always at it. Don't draw conclusions too quickly about what He's doing. Michel de Montaigne (1533–1592) said, "We undo ourselves by impatience," and he was right. Or as Yogi Berra said, "It isn't over till it's over."

God is powerfully at work. Believe what you cannot see; His movements are simply imperceptible to your naked eye.

> The Lord works everything for his own ends—even the wicked for the day of disaster. (Prov. 16:4)

Sometimes Ray and I lead cruises. Each day aboard we get our shoes out of the same closet, our clothes out of the same drawers, and it looks as though nothing has changed. But we're not in the same place! The ship has moved, and we're in brand new waters.

In your family life you really never repeat anything. You may use the same words or motions, but you can't repeat an experience, because God has brought you to a new place. Behind the scenes, unnoticed, He's been moving you to where you've never been before. All things are new. Your family life isn't cyclical but linear.

Professor Albert Einstein used to clap his hands rapidly twice and say to his students, "Between those two claps, you and I moved thirty miles through space."

Every member of your family is changing, becoming—either better or worse. You must see your life together as a journey. Otherwise you tend to handle your spouse or children by repeating what worked yesterday—without noticing that it isn't yesterday anymore. Your partner has changed; so have the children. Everybody's in a new place. What shaped up Kevin when he was eight isn't going to work when he's thirteen.

(A pastor can think he's pastored a church five years when maybe he hasn't. Maybe in reality he's pastored it only one year, repeated five times over.)

In one marriage survey, a man married thirty years said it was almost like being married to a series of different women: "I have watched her grow and have shared with her both the pain and the exhilaration of her journey. I find her more fascinating now than when we were first married."[2]

God is at work in all the kaleidoscoping family transitions: not only in the high points but in the endings, beginnings, detours, dead ends, and in-between times. His powerful tools are not just the promotions and graduations but the failures and firings and losses and sicknesses and shocks and periods of boredom. In them all He's silently, busily, unceasingly encouraging, punishing, shaping.

"The counselor talked to me, and I think I'll take algebra."
"I can't believe I'm pregnant! What went wrong?"
"I did it! I left teaching to go to seminary."
"I do believe I'm losing some hair, right there on top in back. I found it in the mirror."
"The doctor says it's cancer."

In them all, God is tenderly, strongly at work.

"In his heart a man plans his course, but the Lord determines his steps" (Prov. 16:9). And during all His working—all God's silent activity in the disappointments, surprises, delights, irritations—transformations are taking place. "Lord, Thou art the journey and the journey's end."

---

2. Jeannette and Robert Lauer, "Marriages Made to Last," *Psychology Today,* June 1985, 24.

Do you feel as if nothing is happening in yourself, in your family?

I guess so does a lobster, encased in that ridiculous armor. As he grows it even gets crowded inside. But he sheds it fourteen times during his first year of life. Each shedding takes ten days, and each time in the period between shells—when he's naked, exposed, vulnerable—he grows about seven percent.

You feel stifled, unfulfilled? You don't know when you'll break out into change?

Wait for God.

Wait on God.

Wait in God.

Wait with God.

Life is not fixed. Let it happen; don't rush it. "It is God who works in you to will and to act according to his good purpose. Do everything without complaining or arguing" (Phil. 2:13, 14). Keep your eyes fixed on Him, live in obedience as you see it, and then just *be there.*

All you're doing is tending sheep, . . . binding up a scratch, . . . leading to a drink of water, . . .

Year after year after year. . . .

And then suddenly you notice nearby there's a bush on fire.

NOW WORK INTO YOUR LIFE WHAT YOU'VE BEEN READING.

Listen to these words from *Disciplines of the Heart*, and interpret them for your family life:

God is at work in everything. Do you believe that? You won't truly rest and trust if you believe He's only at work in some areas of your life, and the rest is up to you. . . . Are you believing practically at this moment how great He is . . . *for you?* It should begin to relax your muscles even as you read.
"Be still," says the psalm.
"Let your hands hang down," says Hebrews. . . .
Let God be God.

1. Assess the possibility that you've been working at this family thing too hard. Some parents get super-conscientious, hovering, over-directing, tense, driving, unpleasant.

"Be honest in your estimate of yourselves" (Rom. 12:3, TLB).

"On a scale of 1 to 10—10 being obnoxious in the intensity of my parenting as if it all depended on me; 5 being trust in God while I function in obedience as I see it; and 1 being out to lunch, off the scene, totally uninvolved—I rate myself _____."
If you're from 6 to 10, how about reading (or re-reading) pages 84 to 86 of *Disciplines of the Heart?*
2. Have a time of worship and praise to such a God—whether alone or in a group. Read Psalm 86:8–13 in praise and prayer.

 # Your Response to What You've Read

Though no one can go back and make
A brand new start, my friend,
Quite anyone can start from now
And make a brand new end.[1]

The decade of the nineties and then the turn of the century are here. Signs everywhere point to Jesus Christ's soon return—both the ingathering of believers and the growing intensity of wickedness.

And what about you? Do you feel you're emerging into the new era spiritually mature, comfortable in God, coping?

Business Week, in September of 1989, assessed the Western world as "prosperous but edgy, and problems abound, from deficits to crack. . . ." And it announced that Baby Boomers, for all their affluence, are anxiety-ridden! It called them "a generation that carries the scars of its heritage:"

"Even though they never experienced the Depression and have lived in prosperity, they were brought up in the shadow of the Holocaust, the Bomb, and the Cold War," says Richard Easterlin, University of Southern California professor.

"So they tend to worry more and to be more anxious about future security."

---

1. Source unknown.

They worry, for instance, about losing their wealth:

49% are "very concerned" about inflation.

49% are "very concerned" about unemployment.

47% are "very concerned" about foreign competition.

42% are "very concerned" about a decline in economic growth.

31% are "very concerned" about the possibility of another stock market crash.[2]

And they're "very concerned" about threats to the environment, rising crime, the drug war, homelessness, the spread of AIDS, the threat of nuclear war—all real and legitimate concerns. But not many Boomers *act* on any of these concerns—which means the concerns simply degenerate into worry, into a general feeling of malaise, and into a sense of "eat, drink, and have another ski weekend, for tomorrow we die," a vague helplessness in the face of impending doom. They live in fear and not in faith!

Listen to this wistful, wishful "altar call" to the world from secular *Business Week:*

> Emotions other than greed and self-interest—impulses such as altruism or a collective spirit of endeavor—still motivate. . . . There are hopeful glimmerings that people are beginning to respond . . . to some decidedly nonmarket incentives.[3]

This book is an appeal to "nonmarket incentives"—
To restore godly families,
To recoup strong, loving marriages,
To produce again for tomorrow's world happy, hard-working, stable, courageous, God-fearing children,

---

2. Poll of 1,250 adults conducted 25–29 Aug. 1989, by Louis Harris and Associates, Inc. Results should be accurate to within three percentage points. *Business Week,* Sept. 1989, 175.

3. *Business Week,* Sept. 1989, 175.

To please our God and secure His blessings for us and our descendants,
To see repentance, reform, renewal, revival in the family through a return to His *disciplines of the home.*

It's high time.
The world may be in a free-fall avalanche to hell, but you've decided that you and your family aren't going along. As we said, *make the right decisions. Because then your decisions will make you.*

Maybe you've had great damage done already, with bitter memories and unerasable scars—but *start where you are.*

> The journey of
> a thousand miles
> begins with
> a single step

Right now, alone before Him or with your group, why don't you sign your name to new commitments? If you have a marriage partner, hopefully sign together. Then bring your signed book to your final group session for report, dedication, and prayer.

DRASTIC DON'TS:

1. Lord, I'm not going to try to drag my family back to yesterday—that's impossible. But I want to go back to the Bible and courageously follow what You want us to do, together as a family.

_____

your signature

_____

your partner's signature

2. Lord, I'm not going to divorce, from here on, ever. [If you now have a marriage partner] As I did when we married, I surrender my heart again to lifelong commitment, faithfulness, love.

---
your signature

---
your partner's signature

DRASTIC DO'S:

1. Lord, give me the courage to slow down, to truly seek to capture the elegance, the grace, of a more simple life, as You desire for me. Work this in me as I surrender to Your Spirit's control.

---
your signature

---
your partner's signature

2. Lord, I'm going to seek as a lifestyle to stay close to my kids until they're out of the nest. Please make them great men and women of God.

---
your signature

---
your partner's signature

3. Lord, as a loving, faithful Father, please continue to discipline me, and help me to do the same with those You have given me.

———————————————————
your signature

———————————————————
your partner's signature

4. Lord, with the loving firmness of Your Holy Spirit, I'm going to slash the TV watching.

———————————————————
your signature

———————————————————
your partner's signature

5. Lord, I want to model and teach "male" and "female."

———————————————————
your signature

———————————————————
your partner's signature

6. Lord, I want to model and teach respect for authority.

———————————————————
your signature

———————————————————
your partner's signature

7. Lord, I want to seek after the values of Your Word, and model them and teach them to my children.

_____

your signature

_____

your partner's signature

8. Lord, I want to _believe You._ "Help me overcome my unbelief!" (Mark 9:24). I want to live not in unhealthy fears but in joyous trust in You.

_____

your signature

_____

your partner's signature

9. Lord, in these precious years, teach our family to "cocoon"—to love our home, our table, our family altar.

_____

your signature

_____

your partner's signature

10. Lord, please preside over my [our] finances. And as I [we] handle them in obedience to You, I trust You to care for all our needs.

_____

your signature

_____

your partner's signature

_____

Date

If you've made these new commitments to the Lord, would you write and tell me? I'd love to hear.

Your friend in Christ,

Anne Ortlund
32 Whitewater Drive
Corona del Mar
California 92625
U.S.A.

P.S. Turn the page for more books by Ray and me.

Other Books by Anne Ortlund

The Best Half of Life (with Raymond C. Ortlund)
Building a Great Marriage
Children Are Wet Cement
Confident in Christ (with Raymond C. Ortlund)
Disciplines of the Beautiful Woman
Disciplines of the Heart
Discipling One Another
Joanna: A Story of Renewal
Renewal (with Raymond C. Ortlund)
Up with Worship
You Don't Have to Quit (with Raymond C. Ortlund)

Printed in the United States
1879